Center for
Creative Leadership ®

leadership. learning. life.

Standing at the Crossroads

Standing at the Crossroads

Next Steps for High-Achieving Women

Marian N. Ruderman
Patricia J. Ohlott

Center for
Creative Leadership

leadership. learning. life.

JOSSEY-BASS
A Wiley Company
www.josseybass.com

Published by

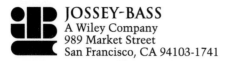 **JOSSEY-BASS**
A Wiley Company
989 Market Street
San Francisco, CA 94103-1741

www.josseybass.com

Jossey-Bass books and products are available through most bookstores. To contact Jossey-Bass directly, call (888) 378-2537, fax to (800) 605-2665, or visit our website at www.josseybass.com.

Substantial discounts on bulk quantities of Jossey-Bass books are available to corporations, professional associations, and other organizations. For details and discount information, contact the special sales department at Jossey-Bass.

We at Jossey-Bass strive to use the most environmentally sensitive paper stocks available to us. Our publications are printed on acid-free recycled stock whenever possible, and our paper always meets or exceeds minimum GPO and EPA requirements.

Jossey-Bass also publishes its books in a variety of electronic formats. Some content that appears in print may not be available in electronic books.

Library of Congress Cataloging-in-Publication Data

Ruderman, Marian N.
    Standing at the crossroads: next steps for high-achieving women / by Marian N. Ruderman and Patricia J. Ohlott.—1st ed.
        p. cm.
    "A joint publication of the Jossey-Bass business & management series and the Center for Creative Leadership."
    ISBN 0-7879-5570-1
    1. Vocational guidance for women. 2. Success in business. 3. Women executives—Psychology. 4. Leadership in women. I. Ohlott, Patricia J. II. Title.
    HF5382.6 .R83 2002
    650.1'082—dc21   2002003580

FIRST EDITION
HB Printing   10 9 8 7 6 5 4 3

A Joint Publication of
The Jossey-Bass
Business & Management Series
and
The Center for Creative Leadership

To Rachel and Joshua,
may you approach the
crossroads of your life with
wisdom, joy, and peace;

To my sister Barbra and
to the memory of my mother, Kathy,
the first two high-achieving women in my life;

To Lew and Tom, love and thanks
for always being there for us.

Contents

Preface

In the course of writing this book, we have merged our personal passions with our professional work. As professionals in the field of leadership development, we realized in the mid-1990s that significant changes were occurring for women managers. We began to have a series of conversations with our colleague Carole Leland, coauthor of *Women of Influence, Women of Vision* and manager of The Women's Leadership Program (TWLP) offered by the Center for Creative Leadership (CCL), and with other leadership development professionals working in the program. They were in frequent contact with high-level women managers from all over the United States, and they shared their observation that women then attending the program were raising issues substantially different from the ones voiced by women in the 1980s.

In the 1980s women attending the leadership program were focused on fitting in and breaking through obvious barriers. They tried hard to be accepted by men and dealt with very blatant acts of discrimination, such as being demoted after maternity leave and being excluded from work-related social functions. These women were organizational pioneers. They were among the first to gain admission to previously male managerial levels, and they were among the first to depart from traditional roles for women in American corporations. Their conversations during the program focused on how to succeed in a man's world, ways to overcome its obstacles, and strategies for breaking the "glass ceiling."

Two things have happened over time. First, although the number of women at the top has stayed relatively low, the number in midlevel management positions has grown significantly. Second, the issues of most concern to managerial women have changed. Women now spend less time on fitting into a man's world and more on the lifestyle choices they confront—choices about *how* to be a woman leader. Choices about whether or not a particular assignment is the right opportunity at the right time. Choices about how much to alter their own leadership style to meet organizational requirements for advancement. Choices about how to keep the costs associated with a managerial life under control. Unfortunately, the existing wisdom on career development provides little specific advice on these issues.

Thus, the women managers who attended TWLP during the 1990s began asking staff at CCL to go beyond existing knowledge and look at the personal and professional choices women face and the approaches they have been taking to address the new realities of their managerial lives. This book is our response to their need.

We endeavored to learn more about the crucial choices managerial women face, with the hope that by studying their inner and outer journeys, we could clarify the experience for others as well as provide some guidance. We wanted to create something that the next wave of women managers could use to understand, validate, and enhance their own experiences. We also sought to help organizations foster the growth and effectiveness of their women managers in this changing environment.

Our Personal Journeys

Growing up as teenagers in the 1970s, we marveled at the burgeoning opportunities for women. We wondered how it would all play out. Would women be able to do it all? This was a time of feminist consciousness-raising and a time of significant social change. All-male institutions like Yale, Princeton, and West Point opened their doors to women. Women started studying law, medicine, and business in large numbers. We were told, Go ahead, you can have a career in any field you choose and can aspire to a position with decision-making authority. From our homes in suburban New Jersey, we watched male executives commute into Manhattan and wondered what that life would be like for a woman executive— and looked forward to a chance to try it one day. Later, each of us moved away from that plan and chose to go to graduate school, one in psychology and one in organizational behavior.

As we began our professional careers, we saw many firsts for women. Sandra Day O'Connor became the first woman appointed to the U.S. Supreme Court, in 1981. In 1983 we saw Sally Ride become the first woman in space. In 1984 we saw Geraldine Ferraro nominated for vice president and heard the women students cheer for her at our university campuses. We also became aware that there were costs associated with the advancement of women as we saw the vicious attacks on Geraldine Ferraro and also on Mary Cunningham when she advanced rapidly at Bendix and was accused of using her feminine wiles to smooth her way. In general, though, we realized that the impossible was becoming possible. But the question of how to handle the choices created by these possibilities never went away. Independently, we each had our own inner dialogue as to what we really wanted out of life: what choices would we make regarding the opportunities available to us?

As leadership development specialists, we tried to find answers in the research literature—for ourselves as well as for our clients. But what we found was a supposedly generic literature on career development based on the experience of white males. We wanted something deeper that went beyond career choices and traditional paths for men. We did find a rich literature on women managers that, although fascinating, emphasized career obstacles, strategies for advancement, and work-family conflict. We also noted that both the popular press and the leadership literature had started featuring articles about women leaders. Despite the many contributions of this literature, none of it answered our need to understand the inner life of women managers. Existing research did not address the goals, opinions, feelings, or doubts of women operating in organizations designed and led by men.

In this book we develop a synthesis of the forces influencing the inner and outer lives of women managers, and we look at how they have addressed the issues these influences raise. It is our hope that the patterns in the needs and life decisions of these high-achievers will enhance understanding in ways that are useful to the decision making of all women in management and those who work with them.

Greensboro, North Carolina   Marian N. Ruderman
March 2002   Patricia J. Ohlott

Acknowledgments

First and foremost, we are especially grateful to the sixty-one women who repeatedly gave us their time to share their stories with us: Your contributions are anonymous but we appreciate the effort and care each one of you individually gave to us in the interviews. Your stories were rich and moving and we appreciate your willingness to trust us with them.

Although only our names appear on the cover of this book, many others at the Center for Creative Leadership contributed to the success of our work. Without them, there would be no book. Most important, we'd like to thank the women who worked on the research team with us. Debbie Nelson, our administrative coordinator, was the glue that kept this project together. She tracked all the interviews, supervised the transcription process, developed all materials, and generally stayed on top of every detail. Kate Panzer read and summarized every interview. Her agile mind helped us to see patterns in the data and organize our thoughts. Sara King, program manager for The Women's Leadership Program for several years, helped us see the research process and the data from the participants' point of view and provided a wealth of insights with regard to applying the findings. Although she joined us late in the process, Julia Biederman Brandon brought to our team a wonderful understanding of the dynamics associated with age and goal setting that greatly enriched our thinking. Sharon

Rogolsky joined us in the last year of our work to share with us her brilliance as a data analyst and editor. Sharon helped us to identify and attend to the flaws in our thinking. She did a wonderful job of helping us to express the subtleties of the data.

Clara Richichi and Carole Sumner also made important contributions to the project by helping us to manage our data and handle administrative details. Interviewing sixty-one women involved a number of individuals; in addition to those women already mentioned, we'd also like to thank Kelly Hannum, Martha Hughes-James, and Davida Sharpe for lending us their interviewing skills.

Many of our colleagues offered us support and advice. Carole Leland persuaded us to undertake the study, and her encouragement gave us the momentum necessary to commit to such a large undertaking. Kathy Kram of Boston University, working with us as an adviser, helped us to clarify our understanding of the data. Talula Cartwright, Wendy Hoelscher, Ellie Johnson, Ancella Livers, Brenda McManigle, Barbara Briggs Popejoy, Sonya Prestridge, and Joan Tavares encouraged us to continue with this work. As the managers and faculty of TWLP, they shared with us their ideas and insights. It was an honor to work with them.

Working on this project was a privilege. We thank John Alexander, Maxine Dalton, Cindy McCauley, Walt Tornow, and Ellen Van Velsor, who gave us the organizational space and resources at CCL to do this. We would also like to thank the many people at CCL who provided logistical support necessary for completion of this project: the research administrative coordinators, the staff of the information center, the assessment services group, the information technology group, and the program coordinators for TWLP. Without all of you this book would not have been possible.

We are also grateful to our editorial team, Marcia Horowitz and Martin Wilcox of CCL, and Cedric Crocker, Kathe Sweeney, Susan Williams, Byron Schneider, Mary Garrett, and Hilary Powers of Jossey-Bass, all of whom provided support and encouragement throughout the process of writing and producing this book. We would also like to thank the three anonymous reviewers whose insights and comments helped clarify our thinking and our writing.

Carol Keck deserves special mention as a colleague and friend to both of us, always confident that we could do this. Personally, we each have many people to thank. Many supported us as we worked on this book.

Marian Acknowledges

My thanks go first to my husband, Lewis Weinstock, for his support and love most of my adult life. I also thank my children, Rachel and Joshua Weinstock, who have brought me incredible joy and happiness. They also inspired some of the thoughts in this book as I reached my own personal crossroads in trying to figure out how to address my goals of being both a good mother and a high-achieving professional. I learned a lot about how to do this from my sister, Audrey Ruderman Levin; she has been my adviser, coach, friend, and confidante my entire life. Thanks to my parents, Carrie and Herman Ruderman, whose love and encouragement helped to make this book a reality.

Patty Acknowledges

I am forever in the debt of Kim Blackwell and her team at Duke University, without whom I might not have been here to write this book. My greatest appreciation is reserved for my husband, Tom Trocano, whose unfailing love, support, and encouragement make all things possible; for my parents, Robert and Kathleen, whom I continue to miss every single day; and for Barbra, Paul, Bob, Jessica, Tyler, Alex, and Bryan, who have loved and supported me in so many ways over the years.

The Authors

Marian N. Ruderman is a research scientist at the Center for Creative Leadership in Greensboro, North Carolina. Her research focuses on the career development of women and the impact of diversity on management development processes. Over the years, Marian has written widely on these topics in CCL reports, book chapters, professional journals, and popular magazines. She is coeditor of *Diversity in Work Teams: Research Paradigms for a Changing Workplace*. Marian has also coauthored CCL's feedback instrument, the Job Challenge Profile. Her published work has been cited widely in the press and has been integrated into leadership programs offered by CCL. In addition, Marian speaks frequently to corporate and academic audiences about issues relating to the career development of women.

Marian is a member of the American Psychological Association, the Academy of Management, and the Society for Industrial and Organizational Psychology. She holds an A.B. from Cornell University and an M.A. and Ph.D. in organizational psychology from the University of Michigan.

Originally from New Jersey, Marian now lives in Greensboro with her husband and two children.

Patricia J. Ohlott is a research associate at the Center for Creative Leadership. Her interest in women's career development began when she was fortunate enough to have the opportunity to work with Rosabeth Moss Kanter while completing her senior thesis at Yale. Patty's current research interests include the career development of women managers and issues relating to the management of diversity in organizations. She was coauthor of a study that looked at gender differences in the management promotion process. She has authored a chapter on developmental job assignments in the Center for Creative Leadership's *Handbook of Leadership Development* and has published extensively in professional journals. Findings from her research are applied in The Women's Leadership Program offered by CCL. She has also coauthored the Job Challenge Profile and contributed to the development of SKILL-SCOPE®, both CCL feedback instruments.

Patty has a B.A. in psychology from Yale University and has done graduate work in business administration, with a concentration in organizational behavior, at Duke University's Fuqua School of Business. She is a member of the American Psychological Association, the Academy of Management, and the Society for Industrial and Organizational Psychology.

Also originally from New Jersey, Patty now resides in Burlington, North Carolina, with her husband and their "child," Molly the Labrador Retriever. Patty is an active volunteer with the American Cancer Society.

Standing at the Crossroads

INTRODUCTION

Standing at the Crossroads

Erin, a sales district manager in a large pharmaceutical company, has steadily moved up the ranks in her organization. She has relocated within the United States several times, and her next move will be an assignment in France. After this European experience, she expects to become one of the vice presidents in the U.S. sales organization. Erin, now forty-three, is currently single. Five years ago she ended her marriage of ten years. She still retains her relationship with her stepdaughter, whom she now calls a "child of the heart."

Erin absolutely loves her job—she finds it very stimulating and creative. She has visited some of the most exciting cities in the world, and she has accomplished things that are a great source of pride for her and her family. Erin feels lucky that in addition to enjoying her job, she is very well paid—it's been a wonderful combination. When she divorced, she did not have the kinds of worries about self-sufficiency some women have. But although Erin enjoys her colleagues, both men and women, she worries that she is too consumed with her career. She wonders what will happen if circumstances change and she loses her job.

Further, Erin notes sadly that she couldn't help but feel a pang of jealousy when her male colleague hugged his wife and children at the airport after their last trip. Would she ever have anyone look so happy to see her walk off a plane? Before she started moving regularly, Erin had a best friend outside work, but for the last ten years all her friends have been colleagues. She still knows a lot of people, but she never really

had a best friend again. Erin would like to make some changes in her
life, but she is not sure what. Although her life is very exciting, she wonders who she is without her job.

Does Erin sound familiar to you? You may have grown up with her
or met her on a plane. She may be you. Lacking an internal picture
of the successful female executive, many high-achieving women
often feel confusion and distress as they wonder how to blend a significant career with their other needs. As women strengthen their
foothold in the executive world, their issues are shifting from gaining access to the boardroom to gaining comfort in the personal life
choices associated with a managerial career.

This is both a change and an expansion of the kinds of struggles typically confronted by high-achieving women. Whereas once
the main issues were gender-related hurdles at work—harassment,
isolation, the constant need to prove oneself, and trying to fit in—
now the emphasis has shifted to the changing contours of life—
choices and trade-offs, the forces that influence decisions, and the
strategies successful women use for constructing meaningful and
fulfilling careers. This leaves many managerial women at a crossroads. Traditional career paths can seem clear but also unsatisfying or impossible to travel, while new paths that allow for a full
and rich life are complex, uncertain, and ambiguous. One woman
told us, "I am not alone in my thinking or my feeling. . . . Hit the
downhill of thirty-five and begin to take a look around you and see
what you've done and you see the corporate grind ahead of you,
and you kind of go, 'I don't know if this is what I want to do forever,' and a lot of women seem to be moving into other areas."

Erin, like many of the women we have come to know over the
years, is now asking such questions as: What does it mean to be a
successful woman manager? Is success simply advancement or can
it be something more? How do I make choices about my life? How
do I merge my career ambitions with my other life goals? Can I be
true to myself and to my organization at the same time? Can I develop my full potential in this job? What am I giving up by suc-

ceeding at work? How do women gain and achieve power? What is an effective political style that will be comfortable for me? How can I be assertive effectively?

Not only do these questions reflect a far different set of concerns from those of previous generations of high-achieving women, many more women these days are asking them. In a 1999 review, University of Connecticut professor Gary Powell concluded that the proportion of women in management had increased dramatically from the 1970s to the 1990s. And according to a 2000 report from Catalyst, a nonprofit organization tracking women's success in the world of work, women hold 12.5 percent of the corporate officer positions in Fortune 500 companies, up from 8.7 percent in 1996. A 1996 report from Catalyst suggests women in corporate leadership positions have busy lives outside work as well: 72 percent of female vice presidents and top leaders in Fortune 1000 companies are married and 64 percent have children.

This is not to say that with the increase in numbers, discrimination has ended; it is simply less absolute. The glass ceiling still exists, but it has cracks, and more people are pressing up against it. And more and more people are noting fundamental problems intrinsic to the design of work and organizations. In *Unbending Gender* (2000), Joan Williams (a lawyer) points out that organizations define the ideal worker as someone who prioritizes work above all other needs in life and never takes time off for caregiving. Organizational systems of advancement and rewards are based on the traditional life patterns of men and as a result are less than welcoming to the traditional life patterns of women, who have been the primary caregivers in the family. It turns out that both formal and tacit organizational career-advancement systems have been based on the ideal of the married male manager. In an article in *Harvard Business Review*, Debra Meyerson and Joyce Fletcher (2000) develop the idea that organizations have been created for men on the basis of men's experiences and ideals. They see gender inequity as a characteristic of modern organizations in which a particular view of masculinity shapes the culture and norms. According to this view, the organization prioritizes work above all else, emphasizes individual achievement and competition, and defines success in terms of financial rewards.

The diminishing of access issues and the increasing numbers of women in the management pipeline are certainly positive developments, but we still know far more about helping men develop as managers than about helping women in this male-oriented environment. Conventional career wisdom based on the experience of married white men does not readily apply to women, and women's careers cannot be seen simply as exceptions to the male experience. Women managers and those who work with them need to know how to navigate in the new terrain, and their organizations should know how to develop women in a landscape that is more accepting of them. Women are at a critical crossroad, where they are faced with choosing the right path for their next steps.

This book aims to draw a map that clearly marks such paths for high-achieving women. It raises the questions that Erin and many others have asked, inspects them carefully, and helps high-achieving women and those who work with them determine the answers.

The Questions We Asked and Why We Asked Them

To better understand the inner landscape of women managers, we studied the experiences of sixty-one high-achievers who attended The Women's Leadership Program (TWLP), a five-day intensive leadership development course conducted by the Center for Creative Leadership (CCL). All were mid- and senior-level managers in jobs of substantial responsibility, with base salaries ranging from the low $80,000s to more than $205,000. They were well educated, with 92 percent holding bachelor's degrees, and the majority were employed by Fortune 500 companies. Ninety-two percent of these women were white, which limits our ability to generalize to women of color. Their average age was forty. Half had children under the age of eighteen, and 71 percent were married or in-volved in a committed relationship. (See the Appendix for a de-tailed description of the research study.)

Viewing the managerial experience as a journey, we wanted to understand where these women traveled, why they traveled there, how they traveled, and the hazards they encountered along the way. We interviewed the participants three times apiece—shortly after they finished the program, six months later, and then one year after the program. In each session we asked what salient issues they were struggling with, how they were responding to them, and which of the responses they made were most effective. To gain additional perspective, we also interviewed the career coaches who had worked with the women during the program to help them understand their feedback. Based on these in-depth interviews and the subsequent analysis, we developed a map of the underlying forces guiding the personal choices and trade-offs in the lives of managerial women.

We have used many stories from the interviews in this book. However, every time we profile someone or use a long example, we have left the essence of the story intact but changed the name and the identifying information. We were also careful to describe experiences shared by more than one woman, to further protect the privacy of those who helped us.

Furthermore, we expanded the research at certain points to in-clude an additional 276 women, to whom we sent a written ques-tionnaire. Their responses allowed us to extend findings to a larger sample.

This book explains the patterns that underlie the dilemmas, choices, and contradictions that influence women's life journeys as managers. It shows how clarifying the patterns in women's lives can be used both to guide women's development and to help them make informed choices about their careers. It also looks at the tur-moil that bubbles in the managerial ranks and addresses what high-achieving women need to know now to further their development toward satisfying, fulfilling careers in the twenty-first century.

A Framework for Developing High-Achieving Women

Understanding five themes can help you make sense of the contradictions that dog high-achieving women managers: acting authentically, making connections, living agentically (that is, as an active agent in one's own destiny), achieving wholeness, and gaining self-clarity. These themes influence the way women approach their careers and their lives. Each has been discussed elsewhere in some other form, but here they are combined in one map for the first time and are discussed in terms of the real-life experiences of managerial women. The five themes are intertwined and change in their relative importance over each woman's life course, forming a sort of tapestry.

Each theme is strong, powerful, and a discrete entity. Woven together by each woman's choices, they create a unique and dynamic image. Age and experience, choices made and paths taken, and effects imposed by the changing world shift the relative importance of the themes over time. As a woman ages and enters different life stages, the themes may shift in a complex pattern, with some becoming submerged and others more visible in a particular part of the overall design. At certain points in life, two or more themes may converge and move together, only to diverge at other times and align with separate parts of the pattern. Each woman weaves her own life's tapestry.

Overview of the Contents

This book is in two parts. Part One contains a chapter for each theme, explaining why the theme matters, what it looks like, its dimensions, how to develop it, and the obstacles to developing it. It includes a "developmental thumbnail" that summarizes the major areas to develop. Part Two looks at the themes from two overall perspectives that illuminate how the individual and the organization can apply an understanding of the themes to enhance their effectiveness. A reference section points the reader to source texts and other literature related to these topics, and an appendix describes the research study in greater depth.

Authenticity, the theme discussed in Chapter One, is the desire to have a healthy alignment between inner values and beliefs and outer behaviors. An authentic person understands her priorities and emotions. She is in touch with what matters to her and has fashioned her life in accordance with those priorities. Many of the women in the study felt they were living extremely authentic lives. For others authenticity was a major problem. Some were in careers they didn't like—involved in the management of widget production when they'd rather be making a more significant contribution to the world, working in places where they had to act unnaturally macho to succeed at work, or trapped in marriages that didn't allow them to be their true selves. These women wanted greater authenticity, and this theme motivated the decisions they made during the year we knew them.

Connection, the topic of Chapter Two, refers to a fundamental human drive—the need to be close to other human beings. Psychologists have long recognized that the need for intimacy is a basic motivator for human behavior. Everyone wants to feel attached or connected to others. We learned that although intimacy was extremely important to most of these women, few had the depth and number of close connections they would have liked. Like Erin, they wanted closer friendships and family ties. Friends at work don't compensate for the lack of a best friend in outside life. And some women didn't even have confidantes at work. They had no one to share concerns with. It was surprising to find a group of adult women so lacking in intimacy, a condition that may well result from living in a time of transition, when women are moving away from roles primarily in the home to roles that balance home and organizational life—a balance that is proving elusive.

Controlling your destiny, the theme of Chapter Three, represents another fundamental human drive: to take initiative on one's own behalf and do whatever it takes to excel in one's chosen endeavor. In psychological terms, this drive is known as *agency*, meaning to act as an agent on one's own behalf. This does not mean being overly controlling; it means needing to be in charge of what happens to you, to the extent that is possible. It refers to intentional actions taken toward achieving a desired goal. This thread manifested itself among the women we interviewed in many different ways. Some spoke of the need to become more comfortable exercising their own authority, while others needed to deal with organizational situations that made them feel helpless. Many felt a need to be more politically sophisticated. Others wanted to learn how to manage the perception that they were too aggressive for women in our society. Many set significant goals for themselves after the program—start new careers, gain greater visibility at work, lose twenty pounds, network more, get a promotion. In taking steps to accomplish these goals, the women demonstrated agency. They began to claim more power and control over their leadership and their lives.

Wholeness, the theme of Chapter Four, represents the desire to unite and integrate different life roles. Wholeness was the most dominant theme in the data. Women very much wanted to have a managerial career that allowed for life outside work that was comfortable, rewarding, and joyous. Some were concerned that they had nothing else in their lives but work—no one to meet them at the airport. Like Erin, they felt lopsided in their development and worried that work loomed too large in their life. Others—mostly mothers of young children—were concerned about wholeness because they felt fragmented and divided. They felt guilty at work when they missed their children, and guilty at home at night dandling a baby—knowing their peers had computers in their laps. They feared they weren't good enough mothers or good enough managers. A desire for wholeness—for having time for a variety of life experiences—motivated many women's growth and influenced steps they took to achieve greater well-being.

The final theme, self-clarity, discussed in Chapter Five, involves understanding one's own motives, behaviors, and values in the context of today's world: the myriad ways organizations treat men and women differently. The women sought to understand how stereotypes and perceptions of women influenced the way their colleagues perceived them. They wanted to understand themselves better—their strengths and weaknesses, likes and dislikes, priorities and values. For some, it was a struggle to distance themselves from situations at work and learn not to overpersonalize work-related problems.

Chapter Six, the first of the two chapters in Part Two, looks at how women differ on their developmental journeys. It discusses the influence of age and life experiences on these journeys. For instance, certain issues are more central at one age than at another. Women in their middle to late thirties tend to be very focused on the multiple roles they have in their lives and to feel dissatisfied with their many competing demands. For them, wholeness and connection are central themes. In contrast, women in their fifties tend to feel more whole and tend to focus on improving self-clarity and enhancing feelings of authenticity.

In Chapter Seven, we take up the organizational implications of our findings. What can organizations do to develop and retain women during this period of societal transition? How can organizations best respond to the transformation of roles for women both at work and at home? Although society has opened up new paths for women, many organizations lag behind in developing climates and policies that support the growth and development of women managers. We describe several cultural shifts and policy changes that will help organizations facilitate the inner and outer development of managerial women.

Using This Book

As you read this book, think about your own situation. Which of these themes resonates with your concerns? What challenges are you facing? Can you use the experiences described here to guide your own journey? The theme that seems most salient for you will reflect your age and current life challenges. For example, whole-ness often means most to women with young children. Women with significant health problems are often most concerned with authenticity, while those in the midst of organizational restruc-turing and realignment tend to think more about how they can re-gain a measure of control over their lives.

The five themes are distinct, but they intertwine and build on each other. In reading the women's stories, it was sometimes hard to tell where one theme ended and another began, particularly because the themes were often combined. For example, a wo-man who wants to get out of a job that prohibits authentic behav-ior may need to take more agentic steps to do so. Developing greater connectedness with others may also require her to initiate those contacts. The themes of wholeness and authenticity were often reflected in the same stories. For each woman, the themes com-bined in different ways for her at different stages in her career and her life.

Although the five themes represent fundamental human needs that people all possess to some extent, everyone can take steps to further develop in these areas if they so choose. The sequence of the chapters reflects the distinct but overlapping qualities of these themes. We start with authenticity because it represents a basic challenge women often face in male-dominated organizations. If you struggle with authenticity and your behaviors are in conflict with your values, needs, and priorities, it is difficult to develop in any other area. The next two chapters address connection and agency, which form building blocks for further development. Wholeness, discussed in the fourth chapter, requires that women have already addressed issues of agency and connection. And the fifth theme, self-clarity, represents a perspective on yourself that evolves over a lifetime.

We suggest you read the chapters in order and follow the way these themes build on each other. Of course, there is no ideal com-bination of themes that would be right for everyone at every point in life, and the strategies that work for one woman may not feel comfortable for another. Use the strategies presented in each chapter as suggestions or starting points in thinking about how you might approach an issue. Then you are likely to find your own strategies or ways to apply the ones we have given you that meet your own needs and express your own individuality.

As you move through the book, it may become apparent to you that you have already dealt with a particular issue for the moment, or that it is not important to you at this time in your life. If you feel strongly that this is the case, it's okay to move on to areas where you feel you require more development. However, each chapter does refer to the others and discusses relationships and interdependencies among the themes, so make sure to at least skim every chapter. You should have a basic understanding of each theme before you move into the second section of the book, which discusses how the themes play out at different stages of life and what organizations can do to help women develop in these areas.

Who Should Read This Book

This book is primarily for high-achieving women. However, we have tried to capture the nature and texture of women managers' developmental concerns so that others could learn how to think about them in their own lives. Anyone else who reads this book, whether that is someone who works with a high-achieving woman or someone who wishes to be one, will learn about the types of career and life issues these women face. They will come away with ideas for guiding the growth and development of high-achieving managers, and will understand how to use the various roles in these women's lives to produce greater wholeness and more effective performance.

What we have learned is relevant to men as well. Expectations have also changed for men. Furthermore, many men today do not support the particular view of masculinity reinforced by organizations. They do not have stay-at-home wives who do all the caregiving. Nor do they want to delegate all caregiving responsibilities to someone else. When we present the themes discussed in this book to predominantly male audiences, the men often comment that they are struggling with similar issues. The themes presented here are relevant to all women and men who desire to both excel in their chosen careers and to have fulfilling lives outside their work.

Human resource professionals can use the book to address the needs of women of high potential. This book will help them to integrate the developmental needs of adult women into the leadership development systems in their organizations. The book also offers guidance both on how to counsel individuals with regard to their own development and how to modify human resource practices so they address the needs of individual women and men as well as of the organization.

Researchers should find the ideas contained here helpful in understanding the complex effects of multiple roles in women's lives. We hope this book will facilitate a new way of thinking about work-family relationships. It offers a means of reconceptualizing the interaction between these two domains so that the enriching and synergistic outcomes of multiple roles are recognized.

Why Is Development for Women Managers Important for Organizations?

A final note. This is not just an issue for individual women. Organizations have very high stakes in understanding and advocating new ways of developing high-achieving women. According to the U.S. Census Bureau, as of 1999, women made up 45.1 percent of the managerial and executive workforce. Contrast this with the 32.4 percent reported for 1983—it's a growing issue. Moreover, women are strong managers. A study reported in *Business Week* found that women score higher than men on measures of desired managerial behaviors (Sharpe, 2000). Given the increasing demand for leadership talent today, organizations can't afford to misunderstand or underestimate the developmental issues facing women in leadership roles.

A particularly serious consequence of ignoring the gendered nature of organizations is the high level of turnover among women managers and executives. This is disturbing not only because it costs companies their substantial investment in these managers' development and because it may hamper efforts to increase organizational diversity, but also because it can hurt an organization's overall effectiveness. Dorothy Moore and E. Holly Buttner found in a study of women entrepreneurs (1997) that one of the key reasons women leave large organizations is that their values simply don't mesh. Thus it becomes critical for organizations to understand what women want out of their lives and how they want and need to develop, so that corporate America does not keep losing this valuable source of talent.

PART ONE

Five Themes for High-Achieving Women

The Woman in the Glass

When you get what you want in your struggle for self
And the world makes you queen for a day,
Just go to the mirror and look at yourself,
And see what that woman has to say.
For it isn't your father or mother or husband
Whose judgment upon you must pass;
The person whose verdict counts most in your life
Is the one staring back from the glass.
She's the person to please, never mind all the rest,
For she's with you clear up to the end.
And you've passed your most dangerous, difficult test
If the woman in the glass is your friend.
You may fool the whole world down the pathway of
   life,
And get pats on your back as you pass.
But your final reward will be heartache and tears
If you've cheated the woman in the glass.

—Author Unknown

1

Acting Authentically

Are you at ease with yourself? Does your life mirror your values? Do you feel true to yourself? Do you put on a false front at work? Do you live by your priorities?

These questions all bear on authenticity, a vital developmental goal in terms of both personal life and leadership roles. Authenticity is not like an MBA, something that you can achieve and keep; it takes constant maintenance and development.

Someone who is authentic has a good understanding of her priorities and emotions. She can sense what is important to her versus what is important to other people, society, or the organization, and can maintain a healthy alignment between inner values and beliefs and outer behaviors. Authenticity is thus a state or condition rather than a personality characteristic.

Why Authenticity Matters

Authenticity matters to both individuals and organizations. For individuals, feeling authentic—that is, feeling that daily actions are in concert with deeply held values and beliefs—builds energy and promotes learning, while the reverse creates inner conflict and turmoil. Adults learn best at work when they feel they can be authentic in that setting. It is hard to develop if you must deny or hide your true values, styles, and desires. Besides fostering learning, authenticity also promotes psychological well-being: how happy you are with your life, how confident you feel, and how accepting you are of yourself. Even if times are difficult, the knowledge that you are behaving in an authentic way can be comforting.

For organizations, having people who feel authentic means having employees who participate fully and honestly and who work in an engaged and enthusiastic manner. Particularly for managers, working in a way that feels untrue saps energy. In addition, inauthenticity can often be recognized by others, becoming a disruptive, negative force in the organization. Organizations that discourage authenticity for the sake of conformity can be creating hidden costs by demoralizing their staff.

Organizations also need to pay attention to authenticity because it correlates with the retention of talent. Indeed, inauthenticity often drives women to leave large organizations. In a survey of senior women executives, the Conference Board of Canada and Catalyst found that 33 percent of women regard the desire to be in an organization with compatible values as a top factor motivating women to leave their current jobs (Griffith, MacBride-King, & Townsend, 1998). In explaining her career moves a manager told us, "I realized the direction I was taking didn't fit within that firm's. I was kind of bucking uphill because of the gender issues. . . . I know that what I wanted required more independence than was possible in that situation." In a study of women entrepreneurs, Moore and Buttner (1997) also found that lack of congruence between personal and organizational values motivated women managers to leave large corporations and start their own businesses.

When Is Authenticity an Issue?

Women managers focused on authenticity most strongly when attending to long-ignored goals and passions, addressing a changing environment, attempting to fit into a male-oriented organization, and responding to a major life event. They worked on being authentic to varying degrees. For some the struggle was strong and persistent. For others it was more a matter of fine-tuning and maintaining an already authentic lifestyle.

The Unlived Dream

Many women want to be novelists, travelers, entrepreneurs, lawyers, artists, and athletes; they have well-developed dreams that they have put aside or restrained in the face of doing something more conventional or coping with financial or familial pressures. As time passes, the unlived dream takes on more prominence and the cost of ignoring it increases. Often it is impractical or difficult to stop everything, switch gears, and pursue a dream—but it is possible to maintain a sense of authenticity without trying to change your life in one fell swoop by introducing small changes.

One woman, for example, dreams of a law practice defending women who cannot defend themselves. Although she enjoys her job, the law remains closer to her heart. She will be disappointed with herself if she doesn't make the move—but as her family's breadwinner she can't stop working and get a law degree. She compensates by volunteering in a women's crisis center. Further, she works toward her dream by building a financial cushion that will eventually let her go to school full time. She is grappling seriously with her long-term goal as she tries to clarify its importance to her life.

Another woman dreams of writing a novel. Working at "just a job" frustrated and drained her, and between work and home life she felt cut off from herself. After much soul-searching, she decided to address the problem by working on the book in her free time. She realized that the book wouldn't get written if it remained a dream—she had to find a way to make it happen. Little by little, she worked on it—jotting down notes, developing an outline, and starting a draft, and also sharing her dream with a close friend. Writing the book is a source of pleasure as well as a way of reaching her inner self.

Both women see the steps they are taking to realize their aspirations as enhancing the authenticity of their lives. Once they realized the importance of their dreams, they took steps to turn them from fantasy to reality.

A Changing Environment

A second type of authenticity struggle occurs when values and behaviors become inconsistent as the environment changes around you. Easy as it is to recognize that you feel uncomfortable, it is often hard to see why. Addressing authenticity requires figuring out what is wrong so the situation can be remedied.

Sophie worked for Atlas Foods for over fifteen years, moving from place to place and advancing in the organization, all within the same functional specialty. She truly enjoyed her job until a new boss arrived, and the work environment changed. Sophie found it difficult to work with him. At first, she felt he simply had a distinctive style, but then she realized it was much more—the new boss was stepping into territory and tactics Sophie felt touched on the immoral and unethical. He had no qualms about misleading others in the organization and pursuing hidden agendas. She realized he lacked integrity. She tried to change the situation and get her boss to revise his approach. It didn't work. She felt betrayed by the environment and she could not reconcile the direction the business was moving with her own values.

To regain a feeling of authenticity, Sophie decided to transfer. It was worth it to her to move to a new city in a different state to be comfortable with the business practices reinforced in the office. "I didn't feel that it was the best personal situation for me to be in," she said. "I wasn't comfortable with it, and it wasn't something I could change or control. So I needed to make the decision that would change it for me, and I couldn't change him."

Sophie might have had other options. Others in a similar situation dealt with it by gaining support for their views and then going to senior management. This can be a difficult move, but senior managers appreciate the honesty—and in some cases improve the climate of the workplace by transferring the boss. The women in the study dealt with inconsistencies in values differently, but they acted when they were driven to do so—and they felt they were living more authentically after the change and that they had grown by taking action.

The boss isn't the only potential problem—employees at any level can violate key values. And the organizational climate itself can simply deteriorate over time. Environmental drift can show up in family and volunteer settings as well, as when spouses grow apart, children grow up and leave home, and volunteer organizations change their mission or clientele. In each case, authenticity requires alertness and willingness to take action rather than go along.

Hiding a Feminine Style

The predominantly male culture of most organizations can impose a third type of struggle: restraining behaviors that seem too feminine so as to fit the mold without appearing more masculine than the men. Women often do what they can to fake being appropriately male for a while, but eventually the feeling of dishonesty catches up.

As noted earlier, based on the lives and expectations of white male executives, most organizations have long-standing norms for autocratic styles of leadership, prioritizing work over family, and aggressive self-promotion (Meyerson & Fletcher, 2000; Acker, 1998; Williams, 2000). But women tend to find these norms that nourished generations of men handicapping. Parts of themselves can't be brought into the organization. Women in this situation strive to be true to themselves within the dictates of the organization, and adaptation isn't always the answer.

Betsy's boss told her that she was "too emotional." She said she wasn't sure what that meant, and he replied that she was too easily upset and too easily provoked into conflict. She responded by pushing back. She acknowledged her emotionality but pointed out that it also led to conflict resolution, innovation, and to a well-functioning team where people felt safe to be themselves. Her team was high-performing and committed. Why was it okay for him to pound his fist to make a point—wasn't that an emotional display, too?

Ultimately, Betsy's boss accepted her argument and gave her more latitude. However, not all women decide to question the boss's values. Instead, they elect to leave.

Lynn worked in a company with a hard-driving workaholic culture and no formal maternity leave policy for managers. Her male peers all had stay-at-home wives. They valued work above all else. Men had been running this group for a long time and young women managers were a rarity. Until she got pregnant, Lynn focused on minimizing the differences between herself and the men, but during the pregnancy it became glaringly obvious that she couldn't be one of the guys. Her boss and colleagues were hostile, grumbling about the time she would be taking off from work. She felt she was treated as damaged goods then—and after her maternity leave it was worse. They made her feel uncomfortable for having taken time off, and her boss transferred her to another satellite location—a move that seemed punitive as it entailed a much longer commute. This led to a reduction of her trust in her boss.

Lynn struggled to present herself in a way that felt real but was also conducive to success. She wanted to bring her whole self—including the fact that she was now a mother—to work, but instead she felt she had to put on a corporate face every day. Continually setting aside signs of being female was difficult and depleting. Covering up her real life cost her energy that she would much rather have put into her work. Ultimately, she opted for a lateral move to a division with a more supportive environment. When she left, her boss viewed her departure as a real loss and did not understand why she transferred. Lynn was disappointed that she felt she had to leave, but the move was essential for maintaining her authenticity.

Of course, this account takes Lynn's views at face value. It would be interesting to know what her boss really thought about the situation and how he would have responded if she had pressed him further on the way she was treated.

As told, Lynn's story borders on bona fide sexual discrimination. Sometimes the situation is subtler. In some places it's practically written on the organization chart that you must be white, male, and married to move up. People who don't pass all those tests are treated skeptically and have to prove themselves. Women often feel left out of social situations and networking opportunities with men; they describe a kind of insidious, invisible force excluding them. It seems essential to join the club—but there's no authentic way to do so.

Women often come to associate maleness with squashing and trampling others on the way to success. They see men taking credit for the work of women and focusing on self-promotion instead of achievement. The prevalence of overtly political behavior leads these women to believe that style and connections trump substance in their organizations, resulting in needless competition.

Further exacerbating the problem, many women are on their own as they figure out how to be themselves and smash through the glass ceiling at the same time. It is hard to develop an authentic business persona if there is no role model demonstrating the skills you need to develop.

A Major Life Event

Authenticity becomes a priority when life changes. A diagnosis of life-threatening illness can shake someone up, prompting review and reassessment of values and behaviors, and women often describe the experience as one of profound learning. With advancing age, good health once taken for granted is called into question—as with one woman whose liver problems led her to reassess her priorities and realign her life accordingly. She realized she was making too many compromises about what mattered to her.

For others, the health crisis of a loved one made them reflect on what was really important. One fifty-year-old said her father's death helped her clarify her priorities and realize she really wants to continue growing in her career rather than prepare for retirement. She said, "I don't feel like I'm finished at work, yet. This is where I want to be . . . there's lots to be done and it's going to be fun." Her father's death motivated her to make a mark at work in a way that was enjoyable. She wanted to leave a lasting impression.

Although we have no hard data, we speculate that the events of September 11, 2001, acted as a catalyst for many adults to reevaluate their priorities. What people thought were major priorities before the event may seem trivial afterward, and the reaction may accelerate the desire to live an authentic life. Stories and anecdotal accounts in newspapers and magazines suggest that in response, many people have refocused their lives to be more in line with their true priorities.

What Does Authenticity Look Like?

One of the defining characteristics of authenticity is a good grasp of priorities and preferences. In our study, the women who expressed the best alignment between their values and behaviors—the ones highest in authenticity—were in touch with what was most important to them. They reviewed their priorities regularly and were open to altering them as needed.

Related to this precision about values was awareness of choices and trade-offs. Women high in authenticity knew the trade-offs they had made and could articulate them: leaving jobs and taking new ones, having children, leaving a bad situation, switching careers, meeting financial goals, moving, divorcing, managing dual careers, balancing work and family, maintaining the relationship between their work group and organization. For example, on the work and family dimension, one woman said she had traded off the speed she moved up in the company for the time she spent with her young children. She believed she would still reach a very high level but that it would take longer with two kids than it would with none, and this was a trade-off she was willing to make. Meanwhile, another woman said she was trading off being on top of every detail with her children for putting in the time necessary for rapid advancement in her organization. Others made trade-offs on financial goals and decided that they would work very hard for a number of years and then retire early. In fact, one woman who retired at the end of the study had explicitly made this trade-off twenty years earlier. Conscious of the implications of her choice, she worked hard for many years to achieve a stable early retirement. The point is that highly authentic women design their lives to suit their greatest priorities.

This awareness of trade-offs was also related to a strong sense of self-determination. These women knew what it would take to be successful in life as they understood success, and they worked toward those goals. They were willing to steer their own course, even when it went against the current. At the same time, they managed to go by their own rules and standards without living outside society; they still fit in. They simply pursued personal definitions of success based on the achievements and values that mattered most to them—as in the anonymous poem that introduces this part of the book, which one of the participants gave us to explain her view of life. The resulting trade-offs can apply both on the job and at home.

Christine made a career change at the age of forty. She was making a lot of money helping a big company manufacture more widgets, but it wasn't satisfying. She wanted to do something with greater meaning and more opportunity to help people, so she resigned and moved out of her urban home to take a lower-paid IT job at a major university.

She had always dreamed of working in an educational setting, and even though she wasn't teaching she felt she was contributing to the university, which had a mission in line with her personal values. In addition, she liked working in a college town, preferring this environment to the city. Christine described the choice not in terms of giving up money but of pursuing a lifelong dream. "It was really important for me to work where I felt like I was doing something meaningful," she said, adding, "I'm sure widgets are very meaningful to the industry, but they don't directly affect human life."

It is also possible to act authentically at work and at home but not be authentic toward yourself. Some women said they wanted to nurture themselves because they valued themselves—but repeatedly ignored their own needs and desires. They made time for everyone and everything but left themselves out of the equation, creating issues of authenticity. For example, they valued exercise but made no time for it. They valued art or music, but were rarely able to indulge themselves.

A final characteristic shared by women of high authenticity was their comfort with decisions made earlier in life. By and large, they had no regrets. They were clear about their values and preferences and had made their decisions accordingly as well as they could at the time, so they did not ruminate about the past. They wasted no energy worrying about what might have been.

How to Develop Authenticity

Authenticity is a fundamental need throughout life, but different ages may call for different techniques for enhancing it. This section outlines some methods women in our study used to develop and maintain their authenticity. Many of these strategies were introduced in The Women's Leadership Program; others were developed by the women themselves. Each was mentioned by several women as helping them sort through issues of authenticity. Exhibit 1.1 provides an overview of the process described in this chapter.

Know Yourself

Work on developing self-awareness of your values and priorities, your likes and dislikes. A key component of acting authentically is understanding what you care about most. On the surface, this

> **EXHIBIT 1.1.** A Developmental Thumbnail for Understanding and Achieving Authenticity.
>
> 1. Work on developing self-awareness.
>   - Prioritize values and understand personal likes and dislikes.
>   - Foster self-awareness of values and priorities.
>   - Visualize yourself five years from now.
>   - Create an actual image of the future.
> 2. Assess your behaviors, choices, and trade-offs.
> 3. Take action to align your values with your life.
> 4. Believe in yourself.
> 5. Get support.

sounds easy to do. In reality, it is not. Life offers many possible priorities and choosing among them means choosing among highly attractive forces.

The list in Exhibit 1.2 provides the basis for a "value sort" exercise that often proves useful. The idea is to rank the values in terms of their importance to you, so as to identify which ones seem most essential. Take a moment to think over these values and add any others that matter to you. Now take a sheet of paper and sort the resulting list into five categories—always valued, often valued, sometimes valued, seldom valued, and never valued—with no more than five in the always-valued category. This may be hard to do, but the always-valued group should reflect your essential self. Focusing on these values, think about how you spend your time. Does your daily life represent what you always value? Are you doing what you sometimes or seldom value at the expense of what is more important to you? How much time and energy do you spend acting in accordance with these values? Do you wish it were more?

In addition to understanding how you prioritize your values, you should also understand your personal likes and dislikes. Many women spend so much time responding to others' agendas at work and at home that they lose sight of their own interests and passions.

EXHIBIT 1.2. How Often Do You Value These Things?

Rate each value on this list according to its importance to you. Add any other values you prize.

Achievement—a sense of accomplishment, mastery, goal achievement

Activity—fast-paced, highly active work

Advancement—growth, seniority, and promotion resulting from work well done

Adventure—new and challenging opportunities, excitement, risk

Aesthetics—appreciation of beauty in things, ideas, surroundings, personal space

Affiliation—interaction with other people, recognition as a member of a particular group, involvement, belonging

Affluence—high income, financial success, prosperity

Authority—position and power to control events and other people's activities

Autonomy—ability to act independently with few constraints, self-sufficiency, self-reliance, ability to make most decisions and choices

Balance—lifestyle that allows for a balance of time for self, family, work, and community

Challenge—continually facing complex and demanding tasks and problems

Change and variation—absence of routine; work responsibilities, daily activities, or settings that change frequently; unpredictability

Collaboration—close, cooperative working relationships with groups

Community—serving and supporting a purpose that supersedes personal desires, "making a difference"

Competency—demonstrating high proficiency and knowledge, showing above-average effectiveness and efficiency at tasks

Competition—rivalry with winning as the goal

Courage—willingness to stand up for one's beliefs

Creativity—discovering, developing, or designing new ideas, formats, programs, or things; demonstrating innovation and imagination

Diverse perspectives—unusual ideas and opinions, points of view that may not seem right or be popular at first but bear fruit in the long run

Duty—respect for authority, rules, and regulations

Economic security—steady and secure employment, adequate financial reward, low risk

Enjoyment—fun, joy, and laughter

Fame—prominence, being well known

Family—spending time with partner, children, parents, or extended family

Friendship—close personal relationships with others

Health—physical and mental well-being, vitality

Helping others—helping people attain their goals, providing care and support

Humor—the ability to laugh at oneself and at life

Influence—having an impact or effect on the attitudes or opinions of other people, persuasiveness

Inner harmony—happiness, contentment, being at peace with oneself

Integrity—acting in accordance with moral and ethical standards; honesty, sincerity, truth; trustworthiness

Justice—fairness, equality, "doing the right thing"

Knowledge—the pursuit of understanding, skill, and expertise; continuous learning

Location—choice of a place to live that is conducive to one's lifestyle

Love—involvement in close, affectionate relationships; intimacy

Loyalty—faithfulness; dedication to individuals, traditions, or organizations

Order—stability, routine, predictability, clear lines of authority, standardized procedures

Personal development—dedication to maximizing one's potential

Physical fitness—staying in shape through exercise and physical activity

Recognition—positive feedback and public credit for work well done; respect and admiration

Responsibility—dependability, reliability, accountability for results

Self-respect—pride, self-esteem, sense of personal identity

EXHIBIT 1.2. (*continued*)

Spirituality—strong spiritual or religious beliefs, moral fulfillment
Status—being respected for one's job or one's association with
a prestigious group or organization
Wisdom—sound judgment based on knowledge, experience, and
understanding

Source: Adapted from R. J. Lee and S. N. King, *Discovering the Leader
in You.* San Francisco: Jossey-Bass, 2001, pp. 60–61. Reprinted with permission.

They forget what brings them joy and contentment. Take another
page and list twenty activities or things that bring you pleasure.
These can be very simple—walking, gardening, practicing an art
or craft, watching television, reading a book, talking to friends,
getting a massage, playing golf, cooking, shopping. Repeat this exercise every two months. Doing this can highlight values that get
lost in the shuffle. You may find you can't list twenty things right
away. For most women, it is easy to get the first ten. The second
ten are more difficult, but it's worth the effort to get in touch with
yourself. If you have trouble, think back—what did you really
enjoy when you were younger? Music? Art? Sports? Theater? Do
you have this in your life now?

A third way to foster awareness of your values and priorities is
by keeping a "gratitude journal." Sarah Ban Breathnach introduced
this idea in *Simple Abundance* (1995), and Oprah Winfrey popu-
larized it on her television show. When keeping a gratitude journal
you take a few minutes every day to record the things for which you
are grateful. Entries might include a wonderful job, a loving husband, good health, loving parents, time to exercise, close friends.
At first it may feel forced to do this. But after a few weeks it will be
much easier, becoming a powerful way to recognize your priorities
and identify which of your many interests, roles, and activities are
most central in your life. Going back and reviewing a few weeks'

worth of entries can help you see patterns that define your life values, helping you sort out what is most important. It will help you see that although you may not be able to have every single thing you want in life, you can and probably do have an abundance.

Visualization is a fourth technique for ferreting out what is most important in your life. Picture yourself five years from now and think about what you will be doing, what you will look like, and who will be with you. Make it a vivid image. Take some time with it. Imagine talking to your future self. What are you like? What are you doing? What advice does your future self give you? This visualized future self can give very strong guidance by showing where you want to go—and sometimes where you dread going. Looking at possible future selves helps in making decisions about the present. Visualization is not always easy but it is worth trying. It can help to do it with one or two friends who are also interested in visualizing their own futures and figuring out what they most value.

A final and related technique involves creating a physical image of the future. At CCL, we have had women make collages using magazines, natural materials, fabrics, and decorations to depict what they want for themselves. Not everyone finds this approach useful, but when it works, it works well. For example, one woman in our study put together a collage of things that gave her joy and used this as a signal that she needed to take more time to nurture herself. She hung it in her dressing room so she would see it morning and evening as a reminder to do something for herself each day and to review what she did each day that gave her joy. Sarah Ban Breathnach describes a means of using collages and imagery as a way of understanding values and priorities in *Something More: Excavating Your Authentic Self* (1998).

Use several of these techniques to understand your essential self better—multiple methods can give you a cross-check and help you identify your most important values and goals. Consciously assess your behaviors, choices, and trade-offs against your values, priorities, and likes and dislikes. Understand what you have already given up and what you are willing to give up in life to get what you want. The women who were highly authentic saw trade-offs not as bad things but as bringing them *closer* to what they wanted most.

Assess Your Behaviors and Values

Look at your values and at what gives you pleasure. Reflect on your hopes and dreams for the future. Look at what you actually do—how you really spend your time and energy. Examine the patterns and trends in your behavior. Are there gaps between what you say you value and what gets your time and energy? Ask yourself what you need to let go of to work toward the things you care about most. Is there something you can trade off? As with the five themes, there are no universal trade-offs. The right choices differ for everyone and even for the same woman at different times. As long as you know what you want in the various realms of your life and what you will and will not do to get it, you can act authentically.

Take Action

We found that women were better at seeing potential trade-offs than they were at taking action to align their lives with their values. Taking action, however, is central to living a more authentic life. It doesn't have to be grand. Some women, like Sophie (see page 20), take dramatic action such as relocating to a new city to get away from an untenable situation. Others pursue a strategy of small wins, taking action on a small scale and gradually improving the alignment between their values and behaviors.

> Maribeth took many small steps to improve the relationships in her life: she stopped going to work on weekends, started spending more time with her children, and curtailed weekend business travel, all in an effort to devote more energy to her relationships. She also helped herself stay focused on her aspirations by reading books on authenticity and surrounding herself with reminders of her goals—putting symbols of her authentic self on display in places where she would see them every day,

to remind herself to act on her goals. Over the course of the year, she grew more comfortable and began to feel she was living an authentic life.

Believe in Yourself

Sometimes acting authentically means going against what everyone else tells you. Do the work to clarify what you care about, then trust your own instincts and support yourself in pursuing those goals. If you know others are likely to try to dissuade you from a course of action, spend time thinking about how to respond—or simply decide to listen and not respond. Authorize yourself to determine what is right by your own standards. At the same time, don't compel yourself to maintain a course of action if it no longer feels right for you. It's okay to change your mind. It's okay to decide that an opportunity, even though it may be very prestigious and represent "the ultimate job" by your profession's standards, is not right for you. Often choices related to authenticity require taking a risk—trust your judgment as to what is right for you.

Get Support

As with many areas of personal development, social support can play a key role in promoting authenticity. If you are making a change in your day-to-day lifestyle, whether it is large or small, it may be helpful to share your goals with others. Other people can help keep you true to your goals by asking how well you are doing, providing feedback and encouragement, and avoiding things that make it harder for you. Asking people to help keep you on track can be especially important when pursuing authenticity, because much of your environment may be rewarding you for the opposite behavior.

Obstacles to Authenticity

Many of the women were quite successful at developing in authenticity during the year of the study. However, family expectations, societal norms, and organizational cultures all acted as forces hampering this process. Every woman lives with a list of shoulds, oughts, and musts in her head. These internal voices represent what we think we must do. Often they serve as guides to good destinations, but not always. In *The Nibble Theory and the Kernel of Power*, Kaleel Jamison (1984) argues that these voices eat away at us, blocking genuine growth and subtly preventing us from growing into our true selves by making us lose sight of what matters most.

Sometimes the internal voices contradict themselves. Many women found that societal norms suggested one course of behavior, organizational norms suggested a second, and familial norms a third. Authenticity can become a struggle when deeply held messages conflict with one another, as they often did for the baby boomers in our study. Baby boomers were born during a time when women were expected to primarily serve their families—to take care of children, maintain the home, take care of elders. But while that norm was in place, feminism and the civil rights movement entered the picture. In 1963, Betty Friedan's *The Feminine Mystique* identified "the problem that has no name" as the problem of women's suppressing their own goals to take care of the needs of others. Feminists encouraged women to attend to their own achievement goals and needs.

As the sixties and seventies progressed, more and more women entered the workforce with the goal of achieving in their own right. Young women were told they could have careers like their fathers—but they still got the message that they should be like their mothers, raise their children, and make their family their number one priority. These types of contradictory messages still exist and make it very difficult for the adult baby boomer to discern her own needs. Acting in an adult manner—in fact, acting in any manner at all—means that someone will be disappointed or some standard will be breached.

In the face of contradictory messages, it can be difficult to search your own soul and figure out what you truly want. Several women told us that even though their parents encouraged them to excel in school, they still tried to mold them into housewives. The conflicting messages clouded their own wishes and needs. As they matured, they still felt they should have careers like their dads and also be good mothers like their moms.

Even if society's norms don't feel contradictory, it can be difficult to live authentically if your dreams run counter to convention. As the women reviewed their pasts, many told us that earlier in their lives they had made significant choices to satisfy others or adhere to convention. Some, for example, selected a particular career because that was what women did at that time. Would-be engineers went to secretarial school in one era; confirmed helpers and relationship managers took up investment banking in another. With the benefit of hindsight one woman told us, "I ended up doing what I viewed was more important and acceptable for the organization rather than what I was really interested in. I made a choice, not necessarily doing what I would have honestly wanted to do, but using other people's values to make my decision." Such choices can affect home life, too.

Connie's marriage was rocky for several years, but she didn't think of divorce until her husband was offered a job that would require relocation. She felt it was imperative to go with her husband, that wives were supposed to do this, and her family and friends all agreed. However, after reflecting on it, she knew it wouldn't work. Although she felt she was swimming upstream to say no, she realized she could not make the move. For many women, this might not sound like a trying choice, but it was extremely painful for someone who was raised to believe that divorce was wrong unless abuse or adultery was involved. Connie felt that to be true to herself she had to go against social convention because continuing this marriage would thwart her own development.

Later in her life, Connie realized she really wanted to be a parent and that she could provide a good home for a child. Though she felt the pull of society's stricture that single motherhood should be avoided at all costs, she intentionally got pregnant. To be true to herself, she felt she had to ignore some of the dictates of society. Connie said that it was extremely difficult to do this, but she felt she could not ignore her deepest desires for the sake of complying with social conventions. Yet she didn't deny all social dictates. She made sure she could support a child financially and emotionally before proceeding and also made sure there would be a father figure in the child's life. Connie conscientiously evaluated the necessary elements of good parenting for her child and concluded that she could provide these as a single parent.

Obviously, internalized norms serve many important purposes. We are not advocating ignoring them and what they represent. Rather, we are advocating understanding these norms as they shape your own behavior and using this understanding in an informed way. And we are advocating that you look at what *you* want to stand for, accomplish, and achieve.

Sometimes going counter to convention is less obvious than it was in the situations we've described here. It can be simply a matter of standing up for yourself in an environment that is subtly non-supportive or inconsistent. Many of the women worked in settings with norms and values different from their own. Several felt blocked from growing authentically in such work environments. Some told us that they worked in organizations that were very hierarchical and had command-and-control styles of leadership. They had more participative styles and felt out of place, questioning their feelings and instincts. There was pressure on them to play the game the way the others did, yet they felt awkward doing so. They felt at a loss trying to fit in with the predominant male culture because their own values—emphasizing participation, empathy, work-life balance, and collaboration—were different.

One well-regarded upper-level manager said her style was different from that of her male peers. The team she led had cooperative norms despite the organization's generally autocratic approach; her people held open discussions, shared power, and made key decisions as a team. Her norms fit her values, style, and view of the workplace. At times she was reluctant to describe her group's decision-making process to others, but she felt that being true to her own leadership standards was critical. She liked the company so much that it seemed worthwhile to stay even though she sometimes wondered if she fit in there. Fortunately, her company valued her good results even if she did use different approaches than the men did. She managed to reconcile her own values with the corporate value structure by demonstrating that she could achieve quality results with a different approach.

In light of the growing numbers of women entering managerial positions, organizations need to consider the ways in which climates and styles block or promote authenticity. Upper-level positions require bringing the whole self to work; blocking top managers from their natural leadership style can be costly. Organizations that require one particular style can unknowingly pose obstacles to authenticity and therefore to productivity.

The organizational emphasis on masculine norms poses obstacles to authenticity for many women managers. As noted in the Introduction, organizations are implicitly gendered. In *Unbending Gender* (2000), Joan Williams discusses the fact that organizations really only reward the "ideal worker," someone who can fully devote everything to work in elite managerial positions. Such managers must be able to work excessively—fifty to seventy hours a week—and be willing to relocate frequently in order to advance. This way of defining the ideal worker has different effects on women than on men; it implicitly puts a burden on managerial women who are also mothers and are likely to prioritize putting time into their caregiving role. As a result, trying to be the highly rewarded "ideal manager" strains women's authenticity by putting them at the center of these conflicting forces. It creates a dilemma in terms of figuring out how to respond.

If you work in an organization that you believe is threatening your authenticity, what can you do? In an interesting book on change in organizations, Debra Meyerson (2001) offers some suggestions for dealing with an environment that has issues with femininity. She suggests a strategy of "tempered radicalism" as a means of improving the fit between a woman manager and her organizational situation. Meyerson describes tempered radicalism as using a strategy of small wins to change the organization from an insider's position: keeping your sense of authenticity in the face of an organization with a nonsupportive culture and creating social change from within. Tempered radicalism provides a middle course between conforming to an uncomfortable environment and stridently opposing it. Meyerson argues that it is possible to advocate for your own values without compromising your standing in the organization. She recommends that women take modest and incremental steps while building alliances and gaining support for a series of changes with cumulative impact. With strategies such as turning personal threats into opportunities, quiet resistance, or negotiation, it is possible to push back on the organization to improve the climate.

Developing authenticity is not easy. A variety of environmental forces create scenarios that make it difficult. Early childhood socialization and current organizational norms such as fierce competition and an individualistic orientation may lead you away from a path that is authentic for you. The task of developing authenticity involves learning to live in a way you find comfortable despite social norms counter to your desired direction. However, the rewards of living authentically are great and make the struggle worthwhile. An authentic life can be active, vital, and committed, while promoting a sense of inner peace.

2

Making Connections

In a very broad sense, connection refers to our need to be close to other human beings—family, friends, community, coworkers. Psychologists acknowledge this need as one of two fundamental human drives that motivate our behavior (along with agency, the topic of the next chapter). Relationships are a source of joy, comfort, and meaning in our lives.

In traditional Western society, a woman defines her identity through attachment and intimacy, organizing and developing her sense of self in the context of her important relationships. Women are expected to act as supporters, caretakers, mothers, maintainers of relationships. In their role as family caregivers, women not only nurture the children but also organize the parties, make the phone calls, and send the birthday and anniversary cards that help maintain the ties with their own family and friends—and those of their spouses. Both clinical observation and psychological research note greater ability in this area among most women than among most men. Other aspects of self—assertiveness, creativity, achievement, and even agency—have long been believed to develop within this primary context. That is, women develop themselves in the process of building, maintaining, and nurturing the important relationships in their lives.

This pattern made it seem likely that the women in our study would have strong, healthy relationships and would feel well connected. And some of them did, but we found a great deal of variation. Those who valued connection often lacked the number or depth of close relationships they would have preferred. Some showed immense concern and compassion for others at work and at home and in extensive networks of contacts—but others seemed to feel no need to work on connections. The latter rarely mentioned networking, mentoring, sharing of hopes and fears with others, or relationships beyond their immediate family. The outside relationships they did discuss often seemed to be solely instrumental, means to accomplish goals rather than sources of support, chances to express themselves, or opportunities to support others.

All the women struggled with the fact that in most organizations, the type of relational work that women have typically been responsible for is not valued. Instead, they and the men they work with are encouraged to strive for individual achievement, often at the expense of other people.

Why Connection Matters

Based on many years of working with women in their clinical practices, psychologists at Wellesley College's Stone Center for Development posit that an inner sense of connection to other people is *the* central organizing force in women's development. In *Women's Growth in Connection* (1991), Judith Jordan, Alexandra Kaplan, Jean Baker Miller, Irene Stiver, and Janet Surrey propose a theory of development of the *self-in-relation*. And in *The Healing Connection* (1997), Miller and Stiver continue the work of developing a new theory that stands in stark contrast to the old male-oriented theories of development, which emphasize independence, autonomy, self-reliance, and individual achievement at the expense of relationships. Instead, they argue that a central developmental task of both women and men is to develop a self *in relation to others*, because relationships provide the foundation for all human development. *Empathy*, the ability to understand and respond to the thoughts and feelings of others, is a prerequisite for a relationship that fosters growth. Creating a mutually empathic relationship requires a high level of cognitive structure, psychological development, and learning. Thus the goal and primary means of development is not isolated individual accomplishment but rather the formation and cultivation of relationships in which both parties are wholly engaged and participating as fully as possible. Such relationships will be both mutually empowering and mutually developmental; both participants derive pleasure from each other's success.

Psychologist Carol Gilligan (1982) suggests that women's experiences of connectedness to others lead to expanded conceptions of self, morality, and relationship. Connection with others helps us see both sides of a situation—the effects of our actions on other people as well as on ourselves. In a wonderful book, *Women's Ways of Knowing* (1986), Mary Belenky and her colleagues suggest that connection is a prerequisite to development for women. The women in their study reported that they preferred to learn from people to whom they felt connected in an empathic and receptive manner, rather than from an "expert" who stood off and could be critical, judgmental, and harsh. For women leaders who value connection, their relationships with others serve three important functions: providing support for oneself as well as for others; enhancing emotional well-being due to social rewards and feelings of joy; and learning, growth, and fostering change that facilitate effectiveness and career success.

Support

One characteristic of a leadership role is that your position limits what people will say to you and what you can reveal. A high-level position requires selectivity in showing vulnerability or sharing confidences.

These limitations may be greater for women than for men at a given level, as women are often stereotyped as more vulnerable than men to begin with. In addition, there may be few if any female peers to get feedback from, socialize with, or learn from. Psychologists recognize that people need to interact with others they see as similar to themselves in ideas, experience, history, and culture. The Women's Leadership Program highlighted this aspect of connection for many of the women we spoke with, because during the week of the program they could benefit from an experience they lacked in their home organizations—being among other women managers and executives.

In a study of the best organizational practices for promoting white women and people of color, Ann Morrison (1992) suggests that such managers experience isolation, prejudice, increased pressure and visibility, and conflict between demands in their personal and professional lives. They may be held to higher standards of performance than their white male colleagues and encounter resentment and hostility from coworkers. These adversities add substantially to the challenges already inherent in management jobs. Although women must face these challenges to continue to develop as leaders, their efforts need to be balanced with appropriate levels of recognition and support from the organization if they are to succeed and advance.

Mary Lynn Pulley (1997) explored why some people who lose their jobs seem more resilient than others. She found that those most likely to experience transformative, positive change— questioning and often revising their assumptions about themselves and their work—were those who had an unusually high capacity for both personal and professional relationships. They had strong support networks before losing their jobs, and they maintained or strengthened their connections during and after the transition. People in their support network helped them open themselves to their experiences and learn from them. Such support can come from a variety of work and nonwork sources, including but not limited to coworkers, professional acquaintances and associations, friends and family, and church groups.

Emotional and Physical Well-Being

Dozens of research studies have documented significant associations between strong personal connections and good spiritual, mental, and physical health. A series of studies by Phyllis Moen and her colleagues at Cornell University (1992) found that women who engaged in multiple roles and, in particular, who were members of volunteer organizations lived longer and were healthier physically and psychologically than those who were not. Other research finds that people active in their religion tend to live longer than those who are unaffiliated; cancer patients who participate in support groups may live longer than those who remain isolated—or at the very least, enjoy a better quality of life. The women we interviewed spoke at length about the rewards they derived from their connections—pleasure, joy, and satisfaction that lifted their spirits in the face of difficulties at work or in other areas of their lives. Women also often used their connections to help them do things to boost their sense of physical well-being. For instance, finding a partner to go to the gym with or joining Weight Watchers helped them accomplish health-related goals.

For years, Meg spent most of her time and energy focusing on the next promotion, the next job, or the next raise. Although her family lived only about an hour away, she seldom saw them. Sometimes months went by before she picked up the phone to call one of them. Her dedication and hard work won her a series of significant promotions at work, along with a "high-potential" tag and a place on the fast track. She occasionally thought about trying to reconnect with her family but postponed doing so, telling herself she would pull back from work "after I get the next big promotion." She missed key anniversaries and birthdays as well as the graduations of her nieces and nephews. Suddenly, a series of catastrophes befell her family. A drunk driver seriously injured her cousin, her father developed congestive heart failure, and her sister, from whom she had long been estranged, was killed in a boating accident. The death hit Meg particularly hard. She realized that the opportunity to reconnect with her sister was gone forever, and she began to question her decision to postpone her relationships as she realized she might never feel established enough in her career to pull back. Meg decided to take the time and reach out to her family now, hoping they would welcome her attempts.

Like many women in high-level positions, Meg is emotionally exhausted; she needs the comfort her family can provide. But relationships don't just provide support when you're down. They can also provide a buffer zone between different areas of your life and help you see difficult situations in new ways.

Although Paula was serious about her career and had attained a significant position, she occasionally took a half day off from work just to spend time with her children, to do something fun with them. She enjoyed this and refused to feel guilty, saying, "It makes me feel good. And so, when I feel good, I think that gives me a lot more energy." Spending time with her children brought her joy and took her mind off her work-related problems. She returned to work reenergized and with a fresh perspective.

Enhanced Effectiveness and Career Success

Despite popular references to the dog-eat-dog business world, extensive research at the Center for Creative Leadership and elsewhere has shown that one of the key executive competencies is the ability to relate to others. In *Working with Emotional Intelligence* (1998), Daniel Goleman points out that a manager with emotional intelligence—that is, with the ability to monitor her own emotions as well as those of others, to discriminate among them, and to use the information to guide her thoughts and behavior—is vastly more effective on the job than one who tries to ignore people's emotional states. Empathy lets a manager relate well to others and make intelligent decisions—decisions that make sense to people even when they disagree.

Another important component of Goleman's concept of emotional intelligence is social skills, which go beyond mere friendliness to involve being friendly with a purpose and moving people toward organizational goals. Managers with strong social skills tend to have a wide circle of acquaintances as well as a knack for building rapport. They are adept at managing teams and influencing others—a manifestation of self-awareness, self-regulation, and empathy combined. Social skills help leaders apply their emotional intelligence to relationships and enhance their ability to handle interpersonal interaction, negotiations, and conflict. In contrast, people who don't realize how they affect other people, don't control their emotional impulses or outbursts, and lack empathy have little chance of developing effective relationships.

Research at CCL has also shown that implementing a business agenda requires good relationship skills. Leslie and Van Velsor (1996) found that derailed executives lacked sensitivity and empathy and were seen as intimidating, arrogant, and abrasive. When they expressed personal charm and seeming concern for others, it was only for purposes of manipulation. As a result of their superficiality, they were unable to develop a strong network of mutually beneficial relationships.

Problems of Connection for High-Performing Managers

As noted earlier, women in executive positions often lack intimate relationships. Some wish to increase the depth and number of their ties, while others feel no need to do so. Women's struggles with connection issues fall into four types: desiring more connection to a group, desiring an intimate connection with another individual, managing a dual-career relationship, and intentionally seeking isolation and distance.

Lack of a Reference Group

Few of the women we spoke with felt part of a community doing similar work, and many were in environments they perceived as hostile rather than safe. They did not feel validated. They wanted to be connected to a group and they struggled with being the odd one out.

In this sense, *connection* refers not to intimacy but to a feeling of belonging to something larger than oneself—to being part of a community. Examples of this type of connection abound in everyday life: Children feel connected at summer camp; adults may join a church, synagogue, or mosque or stay involved with a college alumni group. The support groups devoted to certain illnesses or other problems provide connection because only people who have shared a similar experience can truly understand what others are going through. As well as a sympathetic ear, such groups provide a forum for sharing problems, ideas, strategies, and solutions. Many high-achieving women are surrounded by men and have few if any female peers, which leaves them without community at work.

> Tina had just received some less-than-stellar feedback from her coworkers. As the only woman at her level in an industry with few women at the top, she found it hard to tell if the feedback was valid. Was her performance really subpar? Or were her coworkers biased because she was a female working in a male-dominated industry? Tina lamented the fact that she never had a mentor. She said that when she attended professional meetings, most of the women she met did have someone they looked up to or with whom they had a mentoring relationship. Tina was looking for clarification of the feedback she had received, insight into the way other people perceived her, someone to bounce ideas off of, and someone whose leadership style she could study and perhaps emulate. Prior to receiving the negative feedback, she had believed she could succeed on her own merits and that she didn't need anyone's help. Tina said:
>
> > *What I've learned over this is that I want to help people and there are people out there that want to help just as much as I do. It's just a matter of finding them. So, it's a matter of testing the waters and reaching out and trying to find the right people to help you. I did start opening up to friends and family, whereas before I felt I had to have this strong exterior finish—polished finish. I found that gee, they still like me for who I am. That's not all that bad.*

Tina's friends and family helped her just by listening—providing a sympathetic ear and an independent, neutral viewpoint in a sincere, caring manner. Their acceptance and support helped bolster Tina's confidence, allowing her to laugh ruefully about her mistakes, learn from them, and move on—rather than sitting and ruminating about her problems.

Another woman discussed the satisfaction she derived from being on the giving-support side rather than on the receiving-support side. She was one of about ten women at the management level in her company who established a women's networking group to help themselves as well as women at lower levels in the company, and she found it very gratifying to be able to support and encourage other women. She said they could "understand each other's pain."

Lack of One-on-One Intimacy

The second type of connection many women lacked (even if they were part of a community) was a close, intimate relationship with another individual—a significant other, a very close friend, a family member. They wanted and needed a friend. Almost every woman wanted someone she could feel really close to and let her hair down with without having to worry about the impact of her behavior on her work. And those who had developed intimate relationships expressed their importance to their own well-being and development; they worked constantly to maintain and nurture them.

Elaine was a bright, single professional woman with excellent credentials. She had thus far done very well in her organization, but her only close friend was her sister, who was in the military and had recently been transferred overseas on a two-year assignment. Prior to her sister's departure, Elaine had never felt compelled to develop other close relationships. She and her sister supported each other, and that was enough. Elaine had isolated herself at work as well as in her personal life. She described herself as an independent person who found it easy to meet people but never found it necessary to develop close relationships with them.

Elaine's TWLP career coach told us she was concerned about Elaine's lack of connected relationships, and she anticipated significant emotional trauma for Elaine if anything happened to disrupt her stability at work. She encouraged Elaine to expand her circle of relationships. Elaine recognized the gap in her life as she had been missing the closeness of her relationship with her sister ever since the transfer.

Elaine's situation isn't the only possibility for a single woman.

Kim was also single, but she had two close friends she knew she could always count on. She had regular lunch dates with one friend and met the other at the gym after work nearly every day. If they couldn't get together because of a business trip, they spoke on the phone at least weekly. They knew each other's schedules, shared the intimate details of each other's lives, cried on each other's shoulders. Kim and her friends enjoyed spending time together and motivated and reassured each other. "If you see someone pretty regularly or talk to them regularly," Kim said, "then you can sort of do a pulse check and you know where their lives are too." If she had had a bad day at work, talking with her friends helped buffer her from feeling its effects too strongly; if she stumbled, she knew her friends would be there as a safety net to catch her.

One of the people Mary Lynn Pulley spoke with summed up this sort of relationship quite well: "Knowing, *knowing* that my friends and family are here, it makes the world a less scary place. It's that security that whatever the worst was, I would be OK. I have a number of friends who would send me an airplane ticket and take me into their home. My parents certainly would. I have friends and family that if I were truly sick, they'd come out here in a moment. And I just *know* that" (1997, p. 135).

Unfortunately, a number of the women lacked these types of close connections. They ran from work to workout to all the other tasks they had to accomplish, and they couldn't find the time and energy to cultivate and nurture close, caring relationships. In some cases they seemed to have forgotten how.

Becoming a Couple

The third type of connection issue women experienced stemmed from having to manage a dual-career relationship—to merge their lives and careers with the lives and careers of their spouses or significant others. They had worked long and hard to develop successful, high-power careers. Often they had moved away from friends and family in the process; they prided themselves on being the first in their family or of their circle to go to college, get a graduate degree, or hold a job in a traditionally masculine field. They had attained a measure of financial security, personal and professional recognition, and independence. It was difficult for them to learn to balance independence and dependence in a couple relationship to produce interdependence. Some mentioned difficulty learning how to move from thinking about "I" to thinking about "we." One newly married woman characterized her struggle as follows:

> I think it's the expectations of what I thought marriage would be about, what it would be like . . . and what my Prince Charming dream husband was going to be like is nothing like what I ended up marrying. And I don't mean that in a negative way at all, because I adore my husband. It's just that I'm learning to adjust what I want out of life, and how I measure things. Because my husband was going to be the one who cleaned up after me, he would cook me gourmet meals, he would pamper me from head to toe. That's the expectation I had, and that's not reality. So it's a gradual thing.

As the year went on, her connection with her husband improved, though she still found it difficult. She spoke about how he helped her deal with changes in her workplace:

> He is very much one to say, "How are things going at work today, how did that meeting go, what did you talk about?" I

don't really like talking about those things. But he's very
curious so he's always probing me about these things and he
gets me talking about them. And that is an escape valve
that I recognize, even though I don't want it to be, but it
is a valve and it does really help.

For a few women, long-distance relationships compounded the
difficulty of creating meaningful intimacy in the context of dual
career demands. The time they had with their spouse was limited
and was spent on catching up with each other and, in some cases,
with their children, and that left little time for growth as a couple.

Some women felt they were unable to speak as freely or as openly with their husbands as they could with their friends. They felt
that a good support person needs to be objective while at the same
time acknowledging personal feelings, and they believed their husbands were often unable to do that. One said her husband had difficulty separating his own feelings about an outcome from what
she was feeling. That is, when she was involved in a difficult situation at work, he was unable to distance himself enough to provide an objective perspective because he was so concerned for her
pain. Others felt constrained because the balance of support seemed
unequal—as another woman said, "My husband is supportive of
my career, but he expects me to be a little more supportive of his.
That's a conflict." Although her job was just as demanding as his,
he still expected her to pick up most of the care of their home and
their children. She was reluctant to share work-related problems
and experiences with him because she knew he did not value or
respect her career as much as he esteemed his own.

At other times, connection issues arose when the woman decided to move for the sake of her husband's career. One woman
who had grown up in California and had an extensive network
of friends and family there moved to Ohio with her new husband.
Although she quickly also found a good job, she was deeply lonely
and missed her friends and family in California.

We had a support group there that we were leaving behind. . . . We were moving to an unknown here in Ohio, with no support group, no friends. The hardest part of the move has not been the career part . . . it has been our personal adjustment. That's been one of the hardest things for us, getting reacclimated in a community. Developing that network of friends, not having the support of family or friends that we had in California, having lived there for so long. That has been a difficult transition for us, and we're still working through it.

She and her husband are in the same profession but work in different cities. They live halfway between their jobs to share the burden of commuting—but they were both on the road so much they made no friends near their home. She found no one in her new organization she could relate to, and she was reluctant to make her misery apparent to her husband, who seemed happy in his job. She began flying "home" to California monthly, leaving her husband behind, and she considered returning to California if the situation did not improve. Her sense of isolation threatened her marriage as well as her job. Eventually, she sought out a mentor at work, and other women approached her to mentor them. She joined a church and a community organization. She invited some neighbors to a brunch one Sunday, and she began to limit her trips back to California as she realized they took up time she could be using to develop connections in her new home. Establishing these new connections was difficult for her, but it resulted in significant improvement in her situation and her happiness.

Shutting People Out

A fourth type of connection issue occurred when women purposely closed themselves off from other people or shut down emotionally—most often in response to interpersonal hardship or trauma. Although others regarded such women as uncaring,

aloof, or distant, they were really applying a protective mecha-
nism to keep from being wounded again. Women who had been
sexually harassed on the job or stalked or bothered in their homes
found that the experience affected them profoundly for many years
afterward.

Early in her career, Maureen saw herself as quite open and sensitive to
others. After an experience of sexual harassment at work and a poor
relationship with an overly critical boss, she began to mistrust others as
well as herself. She describes the experience as making her "more
cautious . . . maybe a little more cynical about people . . . more careful
about being open with people," and adds:

It was almost like I was on guard with every person that I met
and not willing to open up and get close to people, especially
men. First of all was because I was afraid of being hurt. It's
taken me a long time to work through that. I think that has inhibited me at work a lot because I'm somewhat defensive and
that has obviously been picked up on. It has also carried over
to my personal life. My husband sometimes asks if I hate men.
I say, "No, I just don't trust a lot of them." And so I have to
deal with those issues.

Maureen worked through these issues with a therapist and she finally felt able to let go of the remaining aftereffects of the trauma when she
attended TWLP. In that supportive group she felt safe enough for the
first time in many years to open up and share her feelings, issues, and
concerns. When she returned to work several coworkers commented
on how changed she was. They saw her as more friendly and approachable and less threatening.

Of course, the women in our study may differ from the typical
American woman. Their lives emphasize individual achievement,
and they are struggling to succeed in highly competitive organizations that are still primarily male-dominated—so it's not surpris-

ing that relationship goals take a back seat to career goals for them. It wasn't clear what was causing the relational breakdown in our findings. Perhaps the drive to get ahead overshadowed the drive to be connected. Or perhaps organizations undervalue the importance of connections and create climates that support individual achievement while stifling relationships.

What Does Connection Look Like?

You may know a woman with a strong network of relationships with other people. What does she do to stay connected with others? Here's an example:

> Cheryl—a middle-level manager, well liked and respected in her organization—has a work mentor who has provided support and developmental assignments for her. She has effective relationships with her coworkers and frequently asks for their feedback on her performance. By connecting with herself, Cheryl feels she is better able to connect with others. As a young manager she was reluctant to mention outside activities or problems at work, but soon she learned that through opening up to others she could connect with people on a more personal level and begin to develop mutual empathy and trust. Cheryl was instrumental in creating a women's professional forum in her company. Her participation in the forum not only brings her the ideas and experiences of more seasoned women managers, it also lets her develop relationships with younger women and pass some of her own knowledge along.
>
> Outside work, Cheryl has several friends she describes as "very close." She feels comfortable telling them just about anything, and she knows they feel the same way about her. She makes it a point to try to meet with one of them for lunch or for drinks after work at least once a week. If she hasn't seen or spoken to them in a while, Cheryl will call them "just to check in" and see how they are doing. Cheryl and her sister and brothers remain close as well, despite the long distances that now separate them. They speak on the phone at least twice a week and exchange regular e-mail messages that often contain photographs

of nieces and nephews. They get together at holidays whenever they can, or they plan to meet at the beach for vacation.

Women with high levels of connection develop and maintain a variety of relationships with family, friends, acquaintances, bosses, peers, and subordinates. Connections play an important role in their self-definition. They see themselves as members of one or more communities, and maintain relationships that are mutually beneficial rather than one-sided. Their management styles are consciously influenced by their relationships with others. They facilitate the development of others and derive personal pleasure and gratification from doing so. They take a supportive and empowering approach to dealing with clients and with those who report to them. In addition, they know how to use relationships to accomplish organizational goals. They are sensitive to the needs of others and gain power through their connections. If isolation is a structural feature of their jobs, they figure out how to actively develop relationships in other ways. During times of change, growth, or difficulty, they know how to get others to support them.

It's not always easy to develop and sustain strong and enduring relationships. Relationships are apt to be the first thing sacrificed when time grows short. Nonetheless, strong personal connections contribute to good health as well as to effectiveness in both personal and professional arenas, and are well worth the effort to pursue.

Using Others to Validate Your Experiences

Through exchanging stories, women learn that they are not alone or crazy. It is empowering to know that what you feel and experience is both real and widely shared.

Corrina had a strong support network; she belonged to a professional women's group within her organization, and made it a point to lunch with colleagues regularly. At the beginning of our study, she had a new job working for a boss who seemed to her to be overly controlling and even at times mean-spirited. He criticized her work constantly, even in areas where she felt particularly skilled. As a consequence, her self-confidence began to erode and she began questioning every action and decision. She became plagued with self-doubt. When we followed up with her on the problem, Corrina told us that meeting with her women's group helped her: "I got to hear the fact that there are other women in the same boat I'm in that have still been able to achieve their goals. It's a very positive thing for me because, quite often, I would look here and think, 'Okay this is just me, I'm the only one struggling through this.' So it was good to find there are other women struggling with the same issues." Some of the women she spoke with reported to the same boss; others had worked for him in the past. All had had problems with him—and the women weren't alone. At lunch one day, a male colleague said he'd had similar difficulties with Corinna's boss. She learned not to take her boss's poor treatment of her personally because he treated everyone that way. Her self-confidence increased as she learned that other people had experienced the same things and had weathered the challenges successfully.

Attending a leadership development program composed only of women was an eye-opener for many of the managers in our study. For the first time, they found how much they had in common with other women managers. This lesson was so valuable that many of them joined or started women's groups upon returning to their home organizations. Women who were encountering difficulties with a boss or husband or who had suffered trauma at work or at home spoke of the value of connection in putting their experience in perspective. Having other positive relationships in their lives helped them stand back and see that not everyone viewed them as a victim or as a problem needing to be solved.

Finding a Community

Lacking a reference group also often meant that women lacked a sense of community—they had no place where they felt they belonged. They had few female peers, and they were tired of being the odd one out. Connections with others in a group or community can help reduce such feelings of isolation and loneliness.

Martha sought out ways to become part of a community wherever she was, and this helped her to be resilient and adapt easily to change. A single woman, over the course of the year we followed her, she switched jobs, houses, and cities, moving to a community where she knew no one. She worried about being accepted and having people like her. One of the first things she did was join a church. Whenever she was not traveling for work, she tried to attend evening mass, which was a real energizer for her. She became active in her church as a coach and spiritual director, becoming close to a whole group of people outside the workplace. Her new workplace was small, and she immediately set about trying to learn the names of all the other employees' spouses and children, because she wanted to be able to connect with people at a level other than their mutual tasks. Martha and some coworkers often cooked together as a group. Sometimes they would stop at a bar after work or have a potluck dinner. The group would join for a pizza lunch and celebrated birthdays with cakes and cards. Weekends were spent with her friends from church. Martha finds peace in the belonging aspect of her connections. She maintains her relationships one-on-one, and she also uses these relationships for guidance in the larger context. Her daily comfort comes from belonging to an organization and from the way she as an individual is a representative of it and a valued member of it.

Women's struggles with connection reflect to a certain extent a larger societal problem. Lack of community has received a great deal of attention in recent years, not just among women but also in society in general. Harvard political scientist Robert Putnam has suggested that the American people are becoming increasingly disconnected from friends, family, neighbors, and society. In *Bowling Alone* (2000), drawing from data from several large-scale social surveys, he argues that the degree to which individuals and communities are connected to each other affects a broad range of outcomes such as health, democracy, school achievement, and crime. Furthermore, social bonds are the strongest predictor of life satisfaction. Interestingly, there appears to be a generational difference in the degree to which people are connected to a community. Robert Wuthnow, in *Loose Connections* (1998), argues that people who came of age in the 1960s or later lacked "great collective events" (such as World War II or the Great Depression) to bolster their shared civic identities. Instead, by setting starkly different norms against each other, the defining events of the last thirty or forty years (such as the civil rights and feminist movements and the cold war) have fostered divisiveness rather than reaffirming common values. Over time, even joining a group became more a matter of individual fulfillment than of commitment or obligation to the community.

As devastating and incomprehensible as they were, the 2001 terrorist attacks on the Pentagon and the World Trade Center may provide a unifying defining moment that touches people in organizations as well as in society at large. In many workplaces, people have come together in ways they never would have considered before. People throughout the United States and around the world felt a deep connection to the victims and their families, even though they had never met, and were motivated to reach out to them and to each other. Some workplaces hosted prayer vigils and memorial services, held community meetings, and provided other ways to help employees connect with and support each other. It has been encouraging to see men as well as women engaged in the very important work of developing empathic relationships. We return to Miller and Stiver, who conclude, "As we move into authentic connections with the people in our lives, we will find more common ground with them, leading us toward an enlarged sense of community and of possibilities for social change. Making connections has implications for the world, not only for our individual lives" (1997, p. 23).

Having a Sounding Board

The women in our survey sought advice and input from others in their networks. Many relied on personal friends, colleagues, spouse, and relatives to help them discuss the ramifications of different choices. When embroiled in a situation where their own perspectives might be clouded by the depth of their involvement and the high stakes at risk, they found it helpful to voice ideas, concerns, dilemmas, and problems to others who were interested and who cared enough about them to listen but were not directly involved in the situation. Sometimes just the process of speaking with another person about the problem provided support and helped the woman clarify her thinking. Even those who spoke only to one person at a time often referred to their circle as an advisory board.

> Sharon started her own business after being laid off from a large retail chain. She was completely content in her new role, feeling creative and free for the first time in years. A few months after she started the business, however, a former mentor called her and told her he had a wonderful opportunity for her in a new company, something that would challenge her and take her out of her area of expertise. Sharon barely considered his offer initially; she was convinced that returning to corporate life was absolutely the wrong thing for her to do. But something inside her said that being so sure of one course of action makes you closed to other possibilities, and perhaps she ought to hear the other side. Sharon decided to create her own "board of directors," people whose opinions she trusted and respected, to advise her on the decision. She chose eight people from her professional life, including another former mentor and people who knew her in different work situations. She told them about the job and about her dreams and goals. Unanimously, every single person told Sharon to take that job. And she says it is the best decision she ever made. Using the sounding board opened her eyes to new possibilities. The new job expanded her horizons, broadened her networks, and set her up for future goals she had not imagined.

Mentoring

Connecting with and helping each other on a one-to-one level was extremely important to many women we interviewed. They spoke about two types of relationships as important facets of remaining connected: finding a mentor for themselves and acting as a mentor for other women.

At least half mentioned that they currently had someone acting as a mentor to them or had had a mentor in the past. Having a mentor or role model helped women validate their experiences and feelings and feel part of a community. Kathy Kram, in *Mentoring at Work* (1988), notes that mentorship serves two key purposes. First, mentors provide development—coaching protégées, protecting them from adversity, enhancing their visibility, providing challenging experiences, and sponsoring career advancement. Second, on a social and emotional level, mentors can provide acceptance, counseling, friendship, role modeling, and personal support. The type of relationship that was most helpful varied as a result of individual needs and organizational circumstances, and it also varied over time and with changes in the participants' situation. Kram's research suggests the most effective mentoring relationships evolve from interpersonal chemistry and mutual attraction. Mentors can be peers as well as bosses, and even people outside the organization can provide some mentoring functions.

Very few women worked in organizations with formal mentoring programs. More often, the relationships began informally, when the woman found someone she admired and wanted to emulate, or when the mentor recognized someone with potential likely to benefit from her knowledge, advice, and counsel. They recognized value in relating to each other. Having more than one mentor was a definite plus; that way a woman did not become overly dependent on the goodwill, prestige, or power of one person.

As a woman moves further along in her career and becomes comfortable in the authority role, she may begin to think about acting as a mentor for another woman—a point we will discuss further in Chapter Six, "Growing Through Life Experience." Managers who were effective at this type of connection often described themselves as conductors or coaches. They liked to be actively involved in the development of other people, whether children or adults—a feeling many women share, and one that is often referred to as a "maternal instinct" or a "nurturing nature." Miller and Stiver (1997) point out that this mind-set encompasses much more. Although these phrases, describing patterns stereotypically attributed to women, convey part of what is involved in a relationship that truly fosters development, the reality is much more complex. The connection has an impact on both parties, and its mutual value should not be underestimated.

Obviously, women who mentor other women can derive fulfillment and satisfaction from the nurturing process. After sharing her program experience with people back in her workplace, one woman told us,

> I came to realize that I like connectedness, and it shows. I find myself attracting others. I never felt myself to be a supporter or a mentor of other women, and I am finding through this experience and this learning what brings me pleasure. I had direct reports that are female, but the network of women and helping women outside of my realm was never something that I pursued. Once in a while we would get together and talk, but I was so busy worrying about my career and my life and all the demons that surrounded me that I never took the effort or made the time to embrace those people. . . . I think I felt in some way threatened. . . . I don't feel that way anymore. I'm getting a lot of people calling me and talking to me, and walking through what's going on in their lives with me, and asking for my advice, and it's very enriching, very fulfilling. I want them to be successful, because I'm okay.

Mentoring may also provide some additional benefits to the mentor. The creativity and youthful energy of a protégée may serve to reenergize the mentor, improve her job performance, and rejuvenate her career. Mentors may also reap the benefit of loyal support from their protégées. Finally, organizations may reward those who take on mentorship roles.

Leading Through Connection

Women managers with healthy connected relationships value their teams and expect that team members will work together and help each other. Effectively managing their connections can lead to greater impact and effectiveness for themselves and their teams. They feel connected to their people and work hard at team building. They recognize that more connections mean more heads working together to solve a problem. More heads translate into more knowledge, a crucial resource for effective decision making and problem solving, and more knowledge leads to greater power.

Women who value connection tend to use participative management. By admitting that they don't know all the answers, they open themselves up to their own growth as well as aiding in the development of others. They recognize that connection at its best is not one-sided but rather is a mutually beneficial, reciprocal process. One woman told us how she began to develop the empathy that helped her create more effective connections with people at work: "I have a very diverse work group. And so when I'm outside of work I'm much more aware of things going on outside of work and I try to interact with a diverse group of people, not only to work on goals or planning but to connect with them on a personal level. And being personally involved with these people outside of work, when I run into someone who might be similar to someone that I work with, my experience with them helps make me more understanding of what their [her employee's] situation is."

Influence and Politics

Although many women shudder at the mere mention of office politics, most have come to accept it as a necessary part of organizational life. Several acknowledged that although they did not like to admit it, the reality was that in their organizations, success was all about political relationships, not production or performance. However, at managerial levels, the ability to influence others is closely tied to performance. "Getting things done" often depends on the ability to influence across department lines and across organizational levels. Access to information and the ability to work behind the scenes with others to anticipate and work around obstacles are critical to long-term individual effectiveness.

In fact, political awareness is high on Goleman's list of key emotional intelligence competencies (1998). The politically astute manager can accurately decipher a group's power relationships and emotional dynamics, identify crucial social networks, and recognize and understand what motivates and shapes the perspectives and behaviors of key constituencies. Goleman further states that outstanding individual managers build bonds with others and balance their own work with carefully chosen favors; they strategically spend time helping others to build accounts of goodwill with people who may have different areas of expertise and who may become critical resources down the line. Such relationships form a reservoir of trust that can be drawn upon to help resolve future problems and provide future opportunities.

One woman who wanted more challenge in her job began looking for a job in a different division of her company. As she quickly learned, "Finding a new job here is based more on relationships and who you know, who can say a good word for you, that kind of thing, versus waiting for a job to be formally announced and then making an application." Research by Robert E. Kaplan and his colleagues (1991) found that highly effective managers are adept at cultivating relationships, whereas less effective managers are often unable to establish, develop, and maintain them. In her final interview, one woman spoke about what she had learned about office politics: "My group recommended some changes we felt would really help the business. There were senior managers who were not necessarily in agreement with some of the changes my group wanted to make, and I learned who the people were I needed to talk with who could influence those senior managers so that they would end up agreeing with what we wanted to do, even though it may really not have been what they agreed with."

Lisa Mainiero (1994) discovered that there is a "seasoning" or subtle maturation process through which women learn intricate political lessons. As they move through the four stages of the process—political naïveté, building credibility, refining a style, and shouldering responsibilities—they become more aware of corporate culture and learn how to work within the system, build alliances and networks, use influence skills, delegate, and overcome obstacles through sheer persistence. Only those who effectively put their learning into practice achieved the highest stage, in which they felt comfortable being the sole woman at the top, could maintain life balance, and were secure and credible enough in their authority role to mentor others.

How Can You Develop Greater Connection?

Many strategies can help you increase your connectedness. Some of them are simple; others are more complex and require greater energy, effort, and time. If you want to develop greater connection, make sure you choose strategies that feel comfortable to you, or your efforts may come across as false and superficial. Some strategies may be more appropriate at different stages of a relationship or for different intents and purposes. Exhibit 2.1 provides an overview of the strategies available.

Map Your Relationships

If you want to develop greater connection in your life, a good place to begin is to identify and evaluate the connections you currently have as well as the connections you may be lacking. The following exercise—based on one used in TWLP and adapted from Josselson (1996)—is designed to help you map your relationships. Participants credited it with helping them to understand their connections to others. Once you have mapped your relationships, use the strategies that follow to work on improving your existing relationships and cultivating new ones.

EXHIBIT 2.1. A Developmental Thumbnail for Understanding and Achieving Connection.

1. Map your relationships.

2. Slow down and take time for people.

3. Join a group.

4. Find a mentor or become one yourself.

5. Reconnect with people from your past.

6. Tap your networks.

Think of a solar system. The sun is at the center, and planets revolve around it at various distances. In the middle of a sheet of paper, draw a circle to represent yourself, at the center of your relational system. Now think about your life. Draw circles in the space outside and around your own to represent your important relationships, which may be to an individual or to an organization. (Some people are part of a group, and it is the group that matters rather than any particular individual in it.) You may also include relationships to people who matter to you internally but who are not there in your physical world, such as someone who has died or someone who is unaware of your feeling about them. Make sure to include relationships both at work and outside work. You may want to put names or other identifying marks inside the circles.

Use the size of each circle to indicate the importance of that relationship in your life. For instance, a small circle indicates that relationship plays a small part in your life right now.

Use the closeness or distance of the circle from your own to indicate the *pull,* or how strong you feel the connection is. That is, place a circle close to yours to indicate that the relationship is solid. If a relationship is very significant and you devote substantial energy to it, draw a very large circle that overlaps your own.

Everyone's map will be unique in detail, but all will take the same general form. Your map might look something like the one in Figure 2.1.

FIGURE 2.1. Relationship Map.

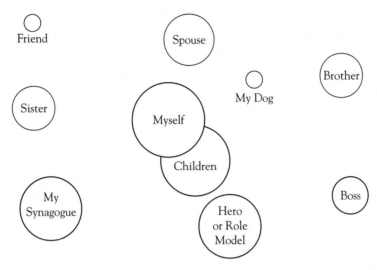

Once you have identified all the relationships that currently have meaning and value for you, look at the areas of your life they represent. What dimensions are covered? Some examples of relationships you may have included are family members, friends, and neighbors; religious, educational, professional, and volunteer organizations; and people you think of primarily as clergy, mentor, boss, subordinate, peer, counselor, or therapist.

Ask yourself why each relationship is important. How does the relationship provide what it does for you, and what does that mean? What effect have different experiences and events had on your relationships? If you feel unsupported and under stress, ask yourself if any relationships are missing that perhaps ought to be there. Are some relationships overemphasized while others are not given enough attention? How much time have you put into resolving conflicts with people who are important to you?

This exercise has several variations you can try. You might want to indicate not only relationships you currently have but also relationships you would like to have. Draw lines from each circle to your own. Use solid lines to indicate existing relationships, and use dotted lines to indicate desired relationships. Is your map more complete now? What will it take to build the new relationships you want? Who can help you? Alternatively, you may want to draw several maps. Draw one that indicates your relationships twenty years ago, another ten years ago, and another five years ago. How have they changed? How would you like them to change in the future?

Finally, you may find it helpful to do this exercise with a partner. Discuss your observations. What is a key awareness for you? Do you have one very large circle overlapping yours and all the rest small and on the outer fringes of the page? Any surprises? Any concerns? How different do you think your map is from those of other leaders in your company?

Pick two or three relationships to pay special attention to, ones with something you want to change. One could be an important relationship with a problem that needs your attention. One could be a relationship that you think could be closer and more fulfilling if you paid more attention to it. Another could be a relationship that does not yet exist but that you would like to have. Set a goal for each relationship and plan a step or two toward each goal. Then schedule that action on your calendar as you would any other commitment. For instance, if the goal is a closer relationship with your brother, then you might schedule a phone call to him once a week. Admittedly this is a simple example, but the important thing is to examine your relationships as things to work on, make the commitments, and schedule them so that you will do something concrete about them.

Slow Down

Lack of time was one of the most common reasons for allowing connections to lapse. Thus the first step toward reestablishing connections is recognizing that connections are important to your personal and professional well-being and effectiveness and that nourishing relationships is a legitimate use of your time.

Establishing connections not related to work allows women managers to exhibit their authenticity as well as to develop better relationships with their staffs. Perhaps it would be worthwhile to leave your children with a babysitter occasionally and go out shopping with friends; shopping trips can be a great way to catch up on what is going on in each other's lives and to share successes and joys as well as trials and tribulations. Or you can slot time into busy weekends for telephoning or e-mailing friends and family who live far away. Take lunch breaks at work so you can spend time in informal conversations with coworkers and employees, or at least make a conscious effort every day to connect with your staff on a personal level by asking questions about their children or what they did for fun over the weekend.

Join a Group

Is there a women's group in your organization? Or a professional-women's organization in your community? Is there a religious or interest group that appeals to you? Make the effort to attend a group meeting. You may have to try several before you find one that seems to fit your needs. Let other members of the group provide you with advice and support, and make sure you return the favor. Participate in the group's activities—outings, meals, socials—as much as possible. Widen your network by inviting others to join as well. If you cannot find a group that suits you, start one!

Establish a Mentoring Relationship

If you are just starting out in your career, or you feel stuck or are looking to make a career change, you may find it helpful to seek out a mentor who can help support you in achieving your goals. Find out if your organization has a formal mentoring program. If it does not, seek out a mentor through informal channels. A mentor need not be your supervisor and may be male or female. Some research suggests that men tend to be more powerful and thus have greater ability to provide career assistance as mentors, whereas women may provide more supportive, psychosocial mentoring functions (McGuire, 1999). Thus, in choosing a mentor, think about what you hope to gain from the relationship. Do you want career advice or just a supportive ear? Do you want the person to be able to provide you with opportunities to increase your visibility in the company? If so, then you should look for a mentor who is likely to have the power and influence to be able to place you in those situations. Or are you really looking for a role model, another woman who seems to have figured out how to fit into the organization yet retain her individuality and femininity while being wildly successful?

Do your research and know as much as you can before making a direct approach, so you can avoid establishing a tie with someone who cannot in fact help you and whose presence in your life may preclude more useful relationships. One woman told us that she asked a number of people in her division to identify the senior manager who might be most open to providing a mentoring relationship for her. She wanted someone who was friendly, approachable, and easy to talk to. After she found such a person and became his protégée, she discovered that he was really in a tangential role and did not hold much influence in the broader reaches of the organization. Thus her chosen mentor was unable to help provide her with opportunities for development or greater exposure to top management.

If you are far enough along in your career to have achieved a measure of success and confidence in your talents and abilities, you may find it useful and rewarding to take on a mentoring role toward someone else. One woman vice president in her early fifties told us, "I think I'm at the stage of life where I'm ready to be in a mentoring role. . . . I would love to be making the trip for some other women a little bit easier. I'm a really big advocate for women in our organization, and I enjoy teaching other women and helping them."

Reconnect with Your Past

Even though it may feel awkward at first, take time to visit or call a friend or associate you've lost touch with. Most people will be glad to hear from you. People who have known you for a long time may know you best and may be in the best position to provide perspective and personal support. They may have earned your trust and respect and may trust and respect you apart from whatever your current job title is.

Jobs come and go, but relationships can endure. At the same time, it is useful to avoid becoming overly dependent on any one connection. Families as well as friends can be abundant sources of support, encouragement, and assistance—and the best way to receive it when you need it is to provide it to others whenever you can.

Tap Your Networks

Chances are you have more opportunities for creating connections than you realize. You may have connections that already exist but that could benefit from some attention and nurturing. Beyond family, friends, acquaintances, and business colleagues, you probably have networks of people who share your profession but work in different companies. These can be particularly effective at giving you relevant but different perspectives on your experiences. Don't neglect or ignore your contacts; work to develop them.

How come I feel so disconnected if this is such a user-friendly world? So many people ask that question that Marcia Byalick and Linda Saslow used it for a book title (1995). For those frustrated by the demands of day-to-day life—with too many roles to fulfill and too many tasks on their to-do lists—they offer a variety of strategies, suggestions, and practical advice for developing richer and more effective connected relationships.

Obstacles to Making Connections

Obviously, lack of time and energy is one important obstacle to developing greater connection. Nurturing relationships takes commitment and work. Busy lives stand in the way of making connections, especially as high-achieving women in organizations can get caught up in a vicious cycle of achievement. They have learned that they have to work harder and be more energetic and productive than men in order to succeed. They begin to feel that they must spend every moment doing something productive, working toward some goal. Phoning a friend or spending a Saturday playing golf with a friend doesn't seem a legitimate use of their time. Meanwhile, male colleagues make time for Rotary Club and Kiwanis meetings, where they continue to expand their personal and professional networks. The first step toward overcoming this obstacle is to recognize that developing and maintaining relationships is an important and legitimate use of your time.

A second obstacle to developing connections is logistical. Women who work in traditionally male-dominated occupations such as engineering may have difficulty finding other women to connect with simply because there are so few women in their industry that there's rarely more than one in any given office. You don't need a large number of women to develop a sense of community, but you do need enough to reduce the sense of loneliness and permit supportive relationships to develop. A study published by Robin Ely in 1994 revealed that women attorneys in law firms with few senior women were less likely than those in firms with many senior women to perceive senior women as role models with legitimate authority. She found that women in male-dominated firms tend to characterize their relationships with other women as competitive in ways that inhibited their ability to work together effectively. A sheer lack of numbers indirectly contributed to their inability to form constructive alliances. If you are in a situation where there are too few women to commune with, you may need to look elsewhere—say, to a professional networking group or trade organization—to develop connected professional relationships.

Finally, organizations can discourage connectedness. Overemphasizing individual achievement in a highly competitive environment makes people focus on the product of the work, rather than the process. As mentioned in earlier chapters, this is a function of the gendered nature of organizational environments that value individual achievement above cooperation, compassion, and connection. As Joyce Fletcher points out in *Disappearing Acts* (1999), many behaviors of connection get "disappeared" and rendered invisible when rewards are distributed. This obviously creates a climate that thwarts the development of skills associated with connection at work.

Within organizations, sexual harassment and discrimination pose significant obstacles to connection. It's impossible to feel part of the group when you are being singled out because of your gender and purposely excluded from opportunities and activities enjoyed by other group members. It's difficult to feel you are part of a community when someone is deliberately doing everything in his power to make you feel uncomfortable. Women who had had these experiences worked hard to redevelop feelings of trust in and connection with other people—but they found it very valuable to do so.

3

Controlling Your Destiny

Early in her life, Susan was a groundbreaker. She always did well in school, especially in math and science courses, and won elections to several leadership positions. She was valedictorian of her high school class, then the first in her family to attend college. She chose a technical career and joined a large pharmaceutical house, unusual choices for a woman from her small rural town. Success continued to come easily—Susan was well liked by her colleagues, and her job performance was excellent. She found a mentor who helped plan and orchestrate her career. She earned a series of increasingly responsible jobs. Knowing she was talented, others came to her to offer opportunities and exciting assignments.

Several years passed, and Susan moved into her first management role, developing a new product. It was supposed to be temporary, a stepping-stone in her career. She did not particularly enjoy the work, but she knew she was learning some valuable lessons and expected to move on soon to bigger and better things at corporate headquarters.

Suddenly Susan's company merged with another, much larger organization. Susan's mentor lost his job, as did others in her network throughout the company. Susan felt her support system was eroding and she was becoming more and more isolated. And the job she'd regarded as her next move was one of those eliminated in the restructuring. Months went by, and Susan grew more and more bored and unhappy in her job. She saw no new opportunities coming her way, and no way to get herself out of her miserable situation. However, she continued to believe that if she performed well she would eventually be rewarded, and to hope that someone in the organization would recognize her situation and her talents and rescue her.

The desire to control one's own destiny is one of the strongest needs of high-achieving women. All the women we interviewed were at least moderately successful. They set lofty goals for themselves and worked to achieve them. Yet, like Susan, almost all had moments when they felt their lives were out of control. The most effective women found ways to pull themselves out of the mire and move on. We refer to this quality of acting assertively on one's own behalf as *agency*.

Why Agency Matters

We borrow the term *agency* from psychologist David Bakan (1966), who was one of the first to identify two basic but opposing human drives he called communion (similar to our connection, discussed in Chapter Two) and agency. He saw agency—the fundamental desire to control one's life and to move to excel—as what motivates us to take the initiative and to advocate for ourselves. From Bakan's perspective, if you are high on one drive, you cannot be high on the other. We depart from that view, as we've found that agency can work in tandem with and complement connection.

Traditional psychological models such as Bakan's start with the premise that the universal developmental task is to build a sense of oneself as autonomous, distinct, and independent from the collective. The drive for self-sufficiency and agency pulls against the drive for communion, which focuses on connection and encompasses cooperation, attachment, and nurturance of others. Agency was associated with qualities seen as traditionally masculine; communion with those seen as traditionally feminine. Thus a woman employing the behaviors of agency—assertiveness, questioning practices that didn't meet her needs, or self-promotion to further

her career—would be seen as inappropriately aggressive, unfeminine, and "out of character." A man using the same behaviors would be seen as strong, masculine, and appropriately powerful.

You need agentic qualities to succeed, especially in the corporate environment. Most people expect nurturing rather than agentic behavior from a woman; when they don't get it they become confused and may be tempted to retaliate. When a woman pushes ahead, putting her personal career advancement ahead of her relationships or the needs of others, she is exhibiting more agency than communion. One woman overheard another instructing her granddaughter, who was nearly a teenager, that no matter how much she disagreed with her father she should not raise her voice nor lose her temper with him, because it was a woman's job to keep the peace in the home and make sure it was a happy place. Even in the twenty-first century, this girl was being taught to value communion over agency. Imagine this young woman years later in her first job, unwilling or unable to assert herself in a competitive environment for fear of rocking the boat or making someone else uncomfortable. In organizations that value initiative, risk-taking, and change-agent skills, she would not advance very far.

In today's turbulent times, where many organizations regard individuals as contractors regardless of job status, no one can assume that someone else will look out for their career. Psychologist Jean Baker Miller (1986) defines agency as being aware of and actively using all one's resources, which doesn't convey overaggressiveness or the other negative connotations for women inherent in Bakan's definition. She also notes the value of communion in the work environment—a point we agree with, as discussed in Chapter Two. Her relational model of growth and those developed and advocated by Judith Jordan and her colleagues (1991) and Joyce Fletcher (1999) propose instead the importance of interdependence in relationships, where people facilitate growth and learning in each other. If two people focus only on their needs for connection, each may become frustrated waiting for the other to take the lead. Taking charge—acting agentically—by acting on a conviction or making a suggestion can be an essential move in a relationship.

Have you ever been in the position of supervising a friend? Suppose your friend developed a performance problem so serious you think of confronting and disciplining or perhaps even firing her. And suppose that she is staying in the job not because she really enjoys or wants it but out of loyalty to you. If you avoid the confrontation because you care for her on a personal level, and she continues to wait and hope the situation may change because she values your friendship and feels she owes you something, your connection can deteriorate as this cycle continues and permeates other aspects of your relationship. By contrast, if you break the pattern by making an active decision to solve the problems rather than letting them fester, you can change things for the better. If you want the relationship or the situation to improve, you must initiate appropriate action to make it happen.

And you can employ agentic behavior without being arrogant and manipulative and sacrificing your relationships. From their years as therapists, Jean Baker Miller and her colleagues (1997) suggest that what matters most for people regardless of gender is that they feel that they are moving, that they can make something happen. This does not mean necessarily resolving everything. It means seeing ways to take action rather than feeling stuck and stagnant—a position that often results in despair, hopelessness, even depression.

People demonstrate agency differently depending on where they are in their careers. At first, achieving your desired position may require you to master particular individual skills and to seek assignments or situations that will allow you to shine above the rest. Later, agency may have to do with the ability to accomplish significant tasks in the context of a rapidly changing organization, to figure out the best way to shoulder new responsibilities, or to determine when it is time to leave a deteriorating job. It may require broadening your span of control to reach wider rather than higher. That is, you may need to connect with people in parts of the organization other than your own who can not only help you get your job done but also help you achieve your career goals. You will need to develop influence skills for situations where you don't have direct authority over people or decisions. Instead of one ladder to climb, you may face a choice among several potential career paths.

Agency also becomes increasingly important over time in the personal realm. For example, as you age, it grows more likely that you will encounter a serious health problem, and getting the best care may require you to develop greater agency. You may have to argue for certain tests or for a second opinion; you may have to search for a physician you can trust. You may find yourself in unsatisfying or damaging relationships (at work or at home) or you may be considering whether to adopt a child. How these situations unfold depends largely on the choices you make and the steps you take. Tough decisions about fashioning your life in accordance with your dreams require agency.

Nancy, director of a large eastern public service agency, faced a problem similar to Connie's (described in Chapter One):

My husband was offered a prestigious job on the West Coast. I did the whole process with him, looked at apartments. . . . I was thinking in the direction of, of course I would follow him. I knew I would have to pursue different aspects of my career . . . and one day I just realized, no, I'm not. I'm going to stay here. I'm going to be on my own. If the marriage is going to make it, we're going to have to make it work from long distance and I'm not going to go. It isn't right. I'm compromising myself, my integrity, my essential being. I'm feeling that I'm going to become dependent in a way that's unhealthy, and I'm not going to be a partner. I'm going to be sort of subordinate, and that was not okay.

Upon reflection, Nancy said this about what she learned:

I think the absolutely best thing about that decision was that I sort of looked into my own soul and realized that if it was going to work, we really had to be meeting one another as partners. And that wasn't the situation. . . . So my advice would be not to be afraid to look into your own soul, and to know that when you do, even if you make a difficult decision, that if you associate an action plan with your vision or with your new understanding of the circumstance, that you'll be able to drive your own life.

For Nancy and most of the other women we interviewed, agency involved working on life plans as well as career plans. Many of the stories we heard involved learning to act on behalf of one's own career, but many others dealt with personal life. Especially for women later in their careers, agency involves thinking about retirement, financial planning, and topics such as "Can I live beyond work?" and "How will I go about doing that?" For many it may mean redefining success. During the year, many women took important steps toward developing greater agency. They grew in personal strength, independence, autonomy, and self-confidence. Women who were learning to take control also grew in self-satisfaction and self-worth.

Ann-Marie was growing increasingly frustrated with the political environment at her company. Different areas refused to work together and "turfism" abounded. Consequently, the organization was experiencing financial performance problems—not to mention serious morale issues. Ann-Marie felt herself withdrawing day by day because she didn't want to deal with the political problems. Yet she felt locked into her job because she had to pay the bills and she didn't want to move. Ann-Marie admitted that she tended to be "reactive." However, after a great deal of introspection and reflection she concluded, "Life is too short to withdraw." Ann-Marie decided to become proactive and try to improve the situation. She developed a program to identify the areas of conflict and cultural differences among the different factions. Implementing the program was risky because it would involve changing the status quo. Ann-Marie knew that as the champion of the program, she risked serious damage to her career if it failed. Further, the issues were emotionally laden, and forcing people to talk about them might disrupt their work even more. Over time and with much hard work, though, Ann-Marie implemented her program, and people who had previously been in conflict were now able to see the overarching goals and began to talk about how they might work together toward achieving them. The company's financial position has improved, and Ann-Marie's success in the job thus far has bolstered her confidence in the ability to make other changes in her life. "If I don't take risks then I'm really not going to learn as quickly or as well I think. Sometimes it's fun to take a risk and win, and sometimes you don't win. But if your track record has more wins than losses, then chances are you're going to not be so afraid of taking those risks."

It is clear that effective agency is important because it helps women achieve career and personal goals. Agency also has a positive and pervasive influence on physical and psychological well-being. This is true for both men and women. Extensive research relates agency to reduced anxiety, reduced depression, enhanced self-esteem, and improved overall health. (See Helgeson, 1994, for a review of these studies.) In Miller's view (1986), developing self-identity in the context of relationships is something everyone must do, male or female. "Growth in connection," as Miller calls it, requires a way of relating in which expressing one's own thoughts, emotions, and ideas promotes forward movement. Rather than talking about agency for the sole purpose of self-advancement, this perspective allows for a dynamic conception of strong, active actions within relationships or connections. In *The Healing Connection* (1997), Miller and Stiver argue that mutual empathy provides the basis for agentic development, allowing people to take action instead of feeling immobilized and ineffective. In cyclical fashion, the resulting assumption of control helps develop mutually empathic relationships.

Struggles over Agency

To find out more about how women acted as agents on their own behalf, we asked them to tell us about key choices they had made in their lives. We also asked about challenges they were currently facing and how they were coping with them, and about their hopes and fears for the future. With these questions we could get a sense of whether these women were more or less agentic in the present than they had been in the past. Our goal was to look at agency as a process, not as a characteristic or trait. It turned out that although many women endeavored to take more control of their lives, their efforts met with varying degrees of success. Why were some successful in taking control while others just seemed to be spinning their wheels? What was happening when agency was used ineffectively? Is it possible to be too agentic?

When Greater Agency Is Needed

Resolving a Difficult Situation. Most often the women who expressed a strong need to develop greater agency had problems at work or in their personal lives. It can be easier to be agentic when things are going smoothly. Women struggled more with agency when they felt stuck in a dull job with little opportunity for growth or in an environment rife with conflict at work or at home. Somehow, they needed to make a change—either in themselves or in their situation. However, making a change often required acting in opposition to what others expected of them and perhaps also violated what they had come to expect of themselves or had become accustomed to.

> Jeanne, a public service manager, had taken the job based on promised opportunities to develop skills she wanted and for promotion as soon as she fulfilled certain requirements. She quickly mastered the requirements and then some, but someone else got the promotion instead. Her boss said she was doing very well and kept assuring her that promotion was "just around the corner." She felt that her boss wanted her there when he needed her but was quick to turn his back on her when he did not. There was a great deal of internal strife in the department and Jeanne felt she had little support and that her options were limited. Jeanne felt angry and frustrated, and it was not at all clear

to her how she could improve her situation. It never occurred to Jeanne that there were steps she might take to change things. Perhaps she might have initiated a productive conversation with her boss or created a task force to identify and address sources of conflict within her department. Alternatively, she might have worked to expand her contacts in preparation for seeking another job.

Many women worked in environments they perceived as downright hostile to them. Bosses or peers were "controlling and meanspirited" and behaved badly toward them and other coworkers. One suggested that in her experience, organizations "set women up" for failure. She felt that men in management believed that women would make life choices away from their careers and toward their families and other personal interests, and this belief led them to deny women key developmental assignments. She said, "It's like a self-fulfilling prophecy. If they're not willing to develop me and give me the opportunities I want and deserve, then I get bored at work and don't feel a sense of accomplishment or achievement of my goals and dreams. I begin to think, 'Is the fight really worth it?'" Several women mentioned harassment so troubling they considered leaving; at least one woman had done so when her organization ignored the continuing harassment. A few women were even stalked or threatened by a coworker.

Lynn (introduced in Chapter One) faced a range of discriminatory challenges. While she was on maternity leave, her boss let her work pile up rather than asking someone else to handle it, and he later transferred her to a location requiring a much longer commute. She chose not to confront her boss or try to change her situation but to persevere and to work even harder; she hoped he would eventually "come around" because her bottom-line results were good and others told her they thought highly of her work. However, the situation did not improve, and the lack of any real relationship between Lynn and her boss made it even harder for her to act agentically. She found the strength to do so only through her relationships with coworkers who helped her see that her boss treated everyone this way; it was not just her problem. Lynn discussed the painful ramifications of her failure to act: "When somebody's telling you you're bad, after a while it starts to wear on you and you get to the point where you start to think that 'I am [a bad manager, a bad person].' He created that self-doubt in me." Looking back, she said she probably should have handled things differently: "There are people out there that have opinions you're not going to change. At some point you have to decide that that's his problem, and I'm just going to move on."

Becoming an Authority. Especially early in their managerial careers, becoming comfortable with personal authority was often a significant challenge. It is more common for girls to be taught to yield to authority rather than to wield it. Women are encouraged to focus more on getting along with and supporting others and working together than on giving direction or creating and enforcing rules for others to follow.

Debra was a housewife for many years. She held several jobs before the birth of her children, but never really had a career. After her children were grown, she decided to reenter the workforce. This was a very agentic step for her, and she worried that she would fail or that no one would want her. But she found a job quickly, and discovered that many lessons learned from managing her home and her family applied directly in her job. She worked hard and performed well. Eventually she was offered a promotion. The prospect of the new job was exciting and a bit frightening—she would be a manager for the first time and would have much more responsibility than in her current job. She was concerned that her coworkers would hate her, now that she was the person with the final say over difficult resource allocation decisions. Debra's husband helped by telling her to stop doubting her ability to make difficult decisions in a rational yet compassionate way. He pointed out all the things she had done in her life that contributed to her managerial skills.

Taking a position of authority has many advantages, but it also increases feelings of vulnerability; in putting yourself out there you are subject to more criticism and the consequences may be higher if you do fail. If you need to make difficult decisions, you may become disliked or resented by those who don't benefit from what you decide. This is often difficult for women to accept. You need some degree of agency to overcome these natural fears. With each level they achieve, even experienced women continue to struggle to accept their own authority. For example, one director—who was in line for a vice presidency—said, "I think people see me as somebody who is confident and authoritative and so forth. . . . I don't at all see myself that way. I see myself as always, kind of, you know, the little kid trying to play dress-up." Over time, successful experience coupled with positive reinforcement through good business results or positive feedback from others helped build these women's confidence in their authority roles. But often it was up to the woman to seek out or create those confidence-building situations for herself.

Negotiating in a Political Climate. Although political behavior is a part of life in organizations, even women who acknowledge it as necessary tend to view it as evil. Some refuse outright to play the political game. One woman told us, "In the past it's been hard for me to try to position myself or align myself with the right people. I'm not going to tell people things just because they want to hear them. I'm not good at being political. I'm not part of the good ol' boy network. And I don't want to be." Another said, "My new boss was very political. And when I say 'very political,' I mean she would do whatever it took to get where she wanted to be or to get others where she wanted them to be—with no thought or consideration to the individuals and the work."

> Phoebe, a senior manager in a multinational consumer product corporation, described her reaction to her organization's political environment as follows:
>
> > There are turf wars which I find unnecessary. And so I withdraw because I don't want to deal with it. We have a lot of empires

*with a lot of people who are not helping the situation. They are
extremely political, to the extent that when they say something
you never know if they honestly feel it or if they honestly mean
it. If somebody tells me "That was a good job" or "You gave a
good presentation," I never know if he really means it or if he is
just trying to curry favor. As a result we are not a team. I still
don't know how to handle those types of people. In the beginning I would have just jumped into the fray of the turf wars.
Now I am trying to take a step back, to try and encourage people to see each other as allies rather than as sabotaging each
other. I try to convey to them that we are the ones responsible
for making a team. I'm trying to change the situation so that the
politics are not so important.*

Phoebe acknowledged that she found this both difficult and painful.
When it became too much to handle, she would withdraw, become
overly cautious in her relationships, or revert to cynicism, all behaviors
likely to hinder her success in the organization.

You may be tempted to follow Phoebe into isolation. However,
awareness of office politics can advance your agency. You need to
know the unwritten policies and procedures and understand where
and how decisions are made. Whose voice carries most weight in
a meeting? Which departments have most control over resources?
Who really wields the influence in your organization? What is
going on behind the scenes? If you know all this, you can capture
opportunities for advancement and develop relationships with
people who are likely to facilitate your goals rather than hinder
them. And you can use political behavior in a way that accords
with your values, though the learning process is apt to be complex.
One woman said, "At first I had an attitude of 'I can do this. I don't
need anyone's help.' But I've learned that I want to help people
and there are people out there who want to help just as much as
I do. It's just a matter of finding them. So it's a matter of testing
the waters and trying to find the right people to help you."

More Agency Is Not Necessarily Better

Until now we have focused on discussing how women struggle to gain greater agency. At the other end of the spectrum are women who overuse agency. As their successes build and they gain power and prestige, they grow arrogant, overbearing, and likely to ignore the needs and feelings of others. Such women exhibit "unmitigated agency," a focus on the self to the exclusion of others (Helgeson & Fritz, 2000). Research has shown that these characteristics and behaviors are correlated with illness, the use of alcohol and drugs, poor mental health, and relatively poor work performance as well.

As we noted in Chapter Two, over the last fifteen years CCL has conducted a series of studies about factors that influence executive success and the reasons executives "derail," or fail to achieve the levels expected of them. A recent review of these studies by Leslie and Van Velsor (1996) found that both those who succeeded and those who derailed possessed remarkable strengths and talents. However, those who derailed possessed at least one "fatal flaw"— a significant weakness that caused them to fail. The most frequent fatal flaw was insensitivity to others. Executives with this problem were described as "difficult to work with." Besides being insensitive, they were overly critical and manipulative, and some became abrasive and intimidating under stress. Talented but insensitive people can often get by until they reach a level where their peers and even subordinates are also powerful and talented. Eventually, micromanagement or alienation of others destroys their support base, and even those who first promoted them are likely to recoil and cut their losses.

Janice focused so strongly on becoming a vice president that she pursued achievement at any cost. She worked long hours, prided herself on never taking vacations, demanded a great deal of her subordinates, and went after what she wanted with a vengeance. Consequently, her division was always near the top. However, her latest performance appraisal included feedback that her colleagues and subordinates saw her as a bully. She was quickly gaining a reputation for leaving broken bodies in her wake. One colleague described her as "pushy, abrasive, domineering, and callous." Others perceived her as "not a team player." A series of conversations with her boss as well as a career counselor helped her realize that ignoring relationships might limit her potential. She began to change her priorities and place greater emphasis on connecting with people. The change paid off; Janice soon started encountering less resistance to her initiatives and enjoying more effective working relationships.

What Does Effective Agency Look Like?

Figuring out how to be agentic and connected at the same time is complex. You may feel you are acting assertive in appropriate ways while others—who are not getting the nurturing and support they normally expect from a woman—see you as overly aggressive. *Elle* magazine recently described a special program for women called "Bully Broads" (Shalit, 2001) as "a remedial program" for women perceived as too domineering or pushy. Participants found that men they worked with were uncomfortable with and even intimidated by women who were strongly results- and action-oriented and who maintained a "no-nonsense, business-like approach." Whether or not they were behaving "appropriately," they needed to find a way to manage other people's perceptions of them. Anyone—male or female—can go too far, be too ambitious. If your image is working for you, you probably don't need to change your style. But be careful not to ignore the signs and signals. If you are acting agentically but don't recognize and respect the human needs of your coworkers enough to fully engage and thus mutually benefit and empower both parties, your career may be headed for difficulty. To be agentic you need a goal, as we discuss in the next section. However, to be agentic *effectively*, you must have both the goal and the means to achieve it. Goals don't exist in a vacuum, and very few can be accomplished without the participation, cooperation, and support of other people.

Clarity of Direction

For short-term goals such as acquiring a specific skill, completing a project, or developing a necessary relationship, you should be clear about where you are going and why. Longer-term goals such as a comfortable and engaging retirement may be more general and evolve and crystallize over time. Long-term goals serve to motivate and to provide a context around which to structure other, shorter-term goals. They let you measure your progress and coordinate action in a particular direction. But having a goal and achieving that goal are different. The latter takes more than prayer and desire, it takes active planning and recognition that there may be many paths toward that goal. Sometimes long-term goals are fuzzy in the beginning. In pursuing those goals, the most effectively agentic women considered both short- and long-term implications of decisions they made along the way.

> Isabelle had trouble getting clear on how to achieve her goals. Upon completing her degree in marketing, she had joined a large manufacturing company that was aggressively recruiting young women. For the first few years she moved rapidly up the management ranks, almost as though someone else was pulling her career strings. When we spoke with her, however, Isabelle was feeling stuck. She'd arranged a transfer to the international area of the business because she was becoming bored with her current work, and international work looked like something different and therefore interesting. When she got there, however, it turned to be essentially the same old work and just as boring as ever. And so, not surprisingly, she continued to be miserable.

Like Isabelle, many women take on goals without clear reasons, only to find that success brings no satisfaction. In fact, such "goals" are not really goals at all, just precursors to goals. They lack the focus and the solid foundation that come from a thorough self-assessment coupled with a sense of the organization's needs.

Clarity of direction means not only knowing what you want but also what you *don't* want. With this knowledge, you can more readily steer clear of paths that may lead you astray. One woman provided us with an example of how knowing what she did not want helped her take charge of her career:

> I had been here and in management for six or seven years. I want to be in a position where I can make things happen, help create the strategy and be involved in decisions that are global for my company. I was getting restless. . . . I'd been doing what I was doing for about four years. When an opening came up at the next level, I interviewed for and was offered the job. My role would have been very different; I would have been spending a lot more time in the community. The hiring manager who offered me the position said he felt like I might be underutilized in the new role, even though it would be a promotion. There was really not much meat to the job, even though it was at a higher level. Much of it was public relations, and I would have had fewer people to supervise. It would have taken me away from my family a lot more and we might have had to move. My family was fully supportive. Of course, I was flattered to be offered the position, but it really gave me the opportunity to take a second look at what I wanted to do in my career. I decided the hiring manager was right, I probably would have been frustrated and unhappy if I had taken that job. I took a gamble and turned it down, because it's not a very popular thing to do with companies. It wasn't going to be fulfilling for me if I wasn't able to accomplish, affect outcomes, and be involved in decisions that were global for the company and make things happen. It turned out to be the right thing to do.

Planful Action

Agentic women *make* things happen rather than letting things happen *to* them, and their choices let them feel in control of life. Women often spoke of "being an advocate for myself versus being a victim," "empowering myself to change," or "being responsible for my situation." The most effective women had well-developed life plans and used short-term objectives to help them reach long-term goals; they were future-oriented. While their goals might shift (or even change dramatically) over time, they kept aiming in a clear direction. But planning alone is not enough; it's also necessary to seek out experiences that will help achieve planned goals. An agentic woman sees her life as a developmental process and takes an active role in it.

Samantha dropped out of college after just two years. She wasn't sure what she wanted to do with her life, but it didn't seem to match her family's expectation: go to college, get married, have children, and have a job but not necessarily a demanding career—to live "happily ever after." She became more and more dissatisfied and restless and finally realized she had to do what was going to make her happy. She traveled widely, pursued a variety of interests and jobs, and eventually married a man with whom she ran a bed and breakfast for several years. Samantha was having fun and found her work satisfying and rewarding, but eventually she knew that she wanted to do something more intellectually challenging, though she still wasn't sure what it might be.

An extended visit home during a family crisis inspired Samantha to rethink her career. She drew on some contacts she had made through her bed-and-breakfast clients to find people to talk with about different career possibilities. She read books and articles about what careers looked most promising in the new millennium. Eventually she knew she would have to return to school. At thirty-two, Samantha decided to resume work on her undergraduate degree—choosing computer science partly because of her interest in the technology but also because she knew it was a growing field, one where—from her bed-and-breakfast experience and her conversations with her contacts—she had identified some business needs she thought she could address. She entered a program that gave her credit for some of her life experiences. She completed her degree quickly and found a job developing software for the hospitality industry. The job allowed her to combine her love of travel, her experience running the bed and breakfast, and her newly acquired computer expertise.

Although her short-term goals changed and evolved along the way, Samantha had always had the goals of completing her education and embarking on a challenging career in the back of her mind. The path she took was unusual, but Samantha could draw on her diverse experiences to help her develop the unique perspective that enhanced her effectiveness at work. She developed a plan and a strategy for achieving her goal and consciously sought out the experiences, information, and education that would help her accomplish it. Because she completed her education later in life, Samantha felt that getting the degree took more conscious planning, and she was able to make the degree more directly useful to her chosen work since she needed it to accomplish her goal. (More on Samantha's story later. . . .)

Taking Calculated Risks

The most effective agentic women sought out experiences that were a stretch for them and required them to do things differently and to learn new skills. Each experience, job, or situation was a stepping-stone designed to bring a future goal closer. Agency requires an ability to extend beyond one's comfort zone, and thus an ability to take some risks. Those with higher levels of agency were able to acknowledge their fears and use them as a reality check rather than an obstacle to taking the risk.

Judith, a middle-level quality control manager, proposed a project to spread new quality control techniques across the organization. She said, "It's going to be an integration where it's not just me leading people in my department who I see every day. It's going to be more of an opportunity to learn more about the organization and more about the different business functions and meet more people and grow more. I'm hoping it will also give me some more visibility, which I think I need." Prior to beginning work on this project, Judith knew she was contributing a great deal, but she was beginning to wonder where her career was going. She explained that many in her company did not understand the role of her group or the value they added. Quality was an afterthought; people came to Judith's group only when they had problems. She took a risk by setting out a new strategic objective whose success would need support from locations all over the world. Judith had to figure out how to sell her idea to top management as well as to the division managers. But she had a solid relationship with her boss, who believed in her and agreed that if she succeeded, there would be major improvements to the business. This made the project seem just a bit less risky. She thought the risk was worth it—and it paid off: "I think that having had the opportunity to establish myself at a higher level by raising this objective and meeting with senior people and presenting the opportunity has given me the groundwork to have them know who I am and what value I add . . . so I feel more secure and established and now I'm thinking that in a couple of years I could strive for and would like to be at the director level."

Self-Awareness

The agentic woman knows what she wants and uses a clear sense of priorities and values to align her plans. She also considers her own sometimes-conflicting wants, desires, and needs up front, and is often not especially surprised that though she might have achieved a long-sought-after goal, she has also had to sacrifice things she truly values in the process.

Anita's career started off well. On her first job, she moved herself and her new husband across country in her quest to fast-track her career. With talent, sacrifice, and hard work, she reached her corporate goals and moved on to still more responsible positions. But ten years and twenty additional pounds later, Anita recognized that having a husband who resented his own sidetracked career, lacking the support of family in her old hometown, and needing to arrange care for aging parents were elements she had neglected to factor into her decisions. What she'd thought was a well-thought-out goal with ample planning only left her growing increasingly depressed. As she was moving closer to her career goals, she was feeling more and more stuck despite her ever increasing salary and prestige.

Contrast Anita's experience with that of Samantha.

Samantha knew that in her newly chosen technical career, she would lose her direct contact with the wide variety of people who had made running the bed and breakfast so enjoyable. She was naturally gregarious and enjoyed talking with people and learning more about them. Her desire for the benefits of a more traditional job precluded her former lifestyle. She consciously chose to postpone that need. If she succeeded in her corporate job, her retirement could afford her a chance to return to innkeeping if she so chose. Samantha and her husband continued to travel and enjoy the atmosphere of staying in bed-and-breakfast inns when they vacationed, and she enjoyed conversing with the other guests and fellow travelers. For Samantha, her agentic striving was made with a conscious awareness of what she might have to give up, at least temporarily.

The most effectively agentic women spent time in self-reflection—at the gym or on the golf course, or by using journals and other tools to chronicle and analyze their thoughts, feelings, ideas, and goals. Understanding your own values, priorities, likes, and dislikes is essential for setting goals that will bring you personal as well as professional fulfillment. Acknowledging risks and fears rather than dismissing them allows you to address them planfully. But the goal is a complex and multifaceted self-awareness—avoiding plans that reflect only part of yourself, which tend to have downsides that cancel out many of their benefits.

Adaptability to Changing Circumstances

Women who used agency well spoke of flexibility in handling challenging tasks, both at home and at work. They developed a wide repertoire of skills that allowed them to respond appropriately in stressful or novel situations, and they could envision a variety of possibilities and generate alternative prospective outcomes. This expanded their flexibility in the face of unexpected contingencies. Despite having plans and goals, they realized that the path to each goal was not necessarily linear, and they often made adjustments along the way.

> Lisa was a product manager in a large electronics firm. When the company restructured, a new position opened up that involved managing a cross-functional team. This appealed to her because she was good at influencing people without exercising direct authority, and she enjoyed being part of and leading an enthusiastic team. The job was in a part of the business new to Lisa, so that besides playing to her strengths, it would allow her to broaden her knowledge base. She let her boss and other key decision makers know she was interested. However, she knew she lacked a core experience that was seen as a prerequisite for the job, so she strategized under two scenarios. She thought about getting the job, and how to make it work without that key experience. And in case she did not get the job, she planned for what she would need to do to make it happen when the next opportunity came along.

When faced with a difficulty or challenge, agentic women often reframe the situation. Rather than feeling blocked or frustrated, they either readjust their goals or find other ways of achieving them. Sometimes they even anticipate obstacles and work in advance to develop strategies to overcome them. They are willing to change themselves as well as their environments.

Flexibility also means choosing your battles. No one can confront every obstacle or pursue every opportunity that comes along. Sometimes compromising in one area can release greater resources in another. Such resources may be as diverse as increased personal energy or gaining allies and partners within the organization. For example, when stymied in the quest for a promotion, it may be tempting to complain—but more useful to sidestep and seek out another opportunity such as participation on an interdepartmental team. This will broaden your exposure in the organization and improve your visibility among decision makers, which will often open up new avenues.

Resilience

A small group of women succeeded against seemingly insurmountable odds. They survived and even thrived despite abuse, harassment, blatant discrimination, and other personal and professional traumas. How did these women emerge victorious? They had so much self-confidence, independence, inner strength, and agency that they knew they could rely on themselves to overcome most barriers to their plans. Instead of letting adversity make them feel powerless, they felt personal responsibility for and control over what happened to them. They wasted little time doubting themselves and rarely cast the blame for their problems on others.

Kristen lost her husband unexpectedly, leaving her to raise their three children by herself. Her company offered her a lateral transfer with the promise of a promotion within two years "when the old man retires." This carrot came with the requirement that she move four hours away from support systems she'd relied on during her adjustment to her family's loss and to single parenthood. Though the offer was not timely, it looked essential to her advancement—and another offer might not be forthcoming. Kristen reluctantly accepted. But well beyond the promised two years, with "the old man" still in place and showing no signs of moving toward retirement, she began to reassess her decision. Although it was never put in writing, it was well known that Kristen had been brought in to eventually take over the department. The "old man" had been rumored to work against women's advancement, and Kristen's recent less-than-shining performance reviews reflected his bias. She knew that if she stayed much longer in this position, no one would want her based on his tainted recommendation. Kristen felt he was hanging on just to spite her. In the meantime, she was dismayed that she was on the road more often. The promised promotion would have required less travel and would have given her more flexibility to attend school recitals and soccer games—but that bright future was not being realized. Kristen arranged to return to her previous position in the town where she had established networks of support. She maintained her professional connections at both locations and eventually did receive the job she'd been promised. By picking up the pieces of her broken dreams and moving forward, Kristen demonstrated agency on both the personal and professional fronts.

Rather than collapsing when faced with personal and professional challenges that might have seemed insurmountable, resilient women like Kristen reframed the situation and found the strength and initiative to master change. They picked up the pieces of their broken dreams and moved forward.

Learning

How many times do you need to fall into the same pit before you learn something that may help you avoid it next time? The ability to glean lessons from experience is a key factor in agency, as it is in developing authenticity, connection, self-clarity, and wholeness. The most effective women expected many challenges and even some failures. Rather than focusing on a failure when it occurred, they saw it as an opportunity to learn so as to approach similar situations differently in the future. Using such experiences for learning greatly reduced regrets about the past.

Jean was responsible for the launch of a new consumer product that was expected to make millions for her company. It was developed and released after just a few customer tests, even though it took the company into an area of business where it had no expertise. After a few months it became evident that the product was a huge flop. Jean's group couldn't meet its quarterly financial goals. Yet Jean believed in the product and persuaded her executive team to give it (and her) a second chance. Once the reprieve was granted, Jean worked hard to understand what had gone wrong. She carefully analyzed their strategy for the product launch. She sought advice from colleagues in her professional network who had experienced both successes and failures in similar business ventures. She looked at what had worked well with other products. Ultimately, she realized the company had not really understood the customers' needs, and the team had never developed a shared view of goals, constraints, and what the product was supposed to be. Once she understood what had gone wrong, Jean was able to regroup. Together, she and her team revisited the market research and made some changes in the product's design, pricing, and advertising. With these modifications, they were able to turn the product around and make it a success.

Jean's career with this company could have been over, but she quickly and agentically took the steps necessary to turn her failure into an accomplishment. She talked with her boss about what she had learned and how to avoid making the same mistakes again. She developed a clear sense of what she would do differently next time. And consequently, her boss had no hesitation about putting her in charge of the next new product launch.

Letting Go

Interestingly, we found that being agentic sometimes meant letting go of things rather than taking them on—removing sources of stress and obstacles that stand between you and your goals. It can also mean recognizing that you can't do everything yourself, and delegating work to others. Both these strategies can help maintain your focus on your high-priority goals.

Jessica, a sales director in a large consumer products organization, was working on trying to relinquish some control and letting other people run with something that was ultimately her responsibility. She found it difficult not to hover over the other members of her team. This took practice. She said, "Eventually I learned about myself that I can still be a key player and not take the lead as much. . . . At the same time, I am not losing accountability, respect, or recognition by communicating and delegating the work so someone else can take the lead." Letting other people do more was tough, but it paid huge dividends in her career. "I had the objective that if I delegated more of the work, maybe I would get an opportunity to spend more time networking and learning more about the organization, throughout the organization, instead of running around putting out fires." Jessica had been pouring so much time and energy into hands-on work that she'd had none left to get out and learn from other people. By letting go of some of her responsibilities, she gained time to build relationships and develop a broader perspective, which was a big step toward her goal of reaching top management in a few years.

Relationships Are Critical

The women most successful at controlling their own lives were those who acted agentically but also maintained good relationships. As they moved from contributor to manager, they increasingly needed to work through others to accomplish their goals. Even those with no direct reports depended on others for information, resources, or support. Although it is possible to be agentic without attending to relationships, women who ignored relationships limited their ability to forge their future.

Jill, director of communications for a manufacturing company, was a master of spin control. When a chemical spill threatened her company's survival, she constructed a series of press releases and corporate media events that turned the potential killing blow into an opportunity. Unfortunately, Jill applied her skill at turning bad news into good to feedback from her own coworkers. When people called her demands on the support staff overly aggressive, she managed to hear it as neutral if not positive. "One needs to be aggressive to be successful," she told herself. Similarly, she shrugged off feedback such as, "Department directors feel Jill does not include them in on decisions that may affect them and that she does not take the time to deal with resistance effectively." Did they not understand the company was in a crisis and she saved their jobs?

Over time, people began to distrust Jill and find her difficult to work with. She accomplished her bottom-line goals, but she also made enemies. The support staff hated to work for her, and key information holders kept quiet because they did not know where or how information they might share with her would be used. Departments developed alternate channels for important information. Before her isolation moved from inconvenience to outright disaster, Jill proudly accepted a new position at a different company. Her reputation (based on her experience with the chemical spill) secured her the job. We can assume that Jill will demonstrate as little caring for her coworkers in this new position as in the last—and cause as much carnage as a result. She may appear to be agentic based on her continued progression, but she is merely staying one step ahead of career demise.

Jill is trying to make it on her own by sheer horsepower, and she won't have much help from others in the process. Effective as she is by herself, she would be even more effective with allies. And if she severs all her connections as she scrambles toward her goals, she risks derailing when she reaches a level where relationships and interpersonal skills become crucial. She has no support system in place to buoy her when she encounters obstacles. Furthermore, she may be missing out on significant opportunities for learning from others who can provide her with different perspectives or experiences that would add value to her decisions and her work.

How Can You Become More Agentic?

Becoming more agentic can be tricky—others may not always view your proactive behaviors positively. The most effective women expressed independent action and self-confidence as they continued to cultivate relationships with their coworkers. Less effective were those who in their extreme self-reliance began to mistrust and perceive others as unworthy of their time and attention. Don't rely on yourself so much that you are unwilling to seek or accept support from others when needed. Exhibit 3.1 provides an overview of the steps discussed in this section.

EXHIBIT 3.1. A Developmental Thumbnail for Understanding and Achieving Agency.

1. Set realistic, specific goals.

2. Develop a plan for achieving your goals.

3. Seek feedback from others and act on it.

4. Remain open to possibilities.

5. Empower yourself.

Set Goals and Adapt Them as Necessary

You need clear and specific goals—some short-term, some calling for a medium-term stretch, and a few idealistic long-term visions—to provide a clear sense of direction. Many of the women we spoke to used a strategy of small wins. They found it helpful to set short-term goals to gain the confidence for greater risks. Remember to reexamine your goals periodically to see if they still seem desirable and attainable. Be prepared to adjust either your goals or your strategies for achieving them as you encounter obstacles. Also spend time examining the congruence of your goals and your actions. This type of reflection is critical because it will help keep you on course.

Most women found it helpful to start with a vision of themselves at some point in the future, or to envision their best and worst working days as a starting place to identify their likes, dislikes, strengths, and weaknesses. Others found it helpful to think about questions such as, "If you knew you were going to leave your job in a year, how would you choose to spend that time? What do you want to be remembered for? What specific action will you take in the next week to help move you closer to that goal?" One woman wrote up a plan for her goals and gave the letter to a friend with a request to mail it back in a year to help her get back on track should she lose sight of her goals. Other women found it helpful to check in more frequently, setting aside time each week to measure progress (either alone or with a close friend) and revise their goals as needed.

Try the following exercise to begin to identify and articulate your goals:

> Examine your résumé as it is right now. (If it's been sitting around for a while, bring it up to date first.) Then rewrite it as you would like it to look five years from now. Think about what you need to do to get there.
>
> - Identify three things you can do that will help move you toward your desired condition.
>
> - Develop a plan, a set of measures, and a process for follow-up and reinspiration.
>
> - Write a letter to yourself detailing your plans.
>
> - Talk your plans over with a friend and commit to carrying them out and to checking in with your friend and yourself at set intervals.

This exercise addresses career goals. You may also want to think more broadly about life goals. You can use a similar technique, but begin with a different vision. Visualize yourself at some time in the future (five, ten, twenty-five years). Where will you be? What will you be like at that age? Develop a list of everything you want to do by then, in any part of your life—think of educational, intellectual, societal, health, spiritual, family, career, lifestyle, financial, recreational, and relationship goals. Which are more important to you? Which less so? Which are short-term goals? Which are long-term, and which involve a combination of long- and short-term elements? Think about what you need to achieve them.

Have a Plan and Update It as Conditions Change

Once you know what you want, you can make a plan to get it. Goals remain dreams in the absence of a clear plan. Goals that are more of a stretch may require more planning and smaller steps. An executive-level job may demand an advanced degree or specific experiences or assignments. And simpler goals such as losing ten pounds also take planning—follow the latest diet guru, go to a spa for a week, join a gym. Even with a nebulous goal like a desire to see the world, you're better off with a strategy or plan of action.

Reflecting on the times when they felt less agentic, women often described periods of waiting. For what? With the chuckle that only hindsight can bring, the general answer was for someone else to rescue them. They knew they wanted a change, but had no plan to get out of the current bind, let alone what direction to go once they were out. They were paralyzed.

Even the clearest goal and best-thought-out plan may encounter some rough spots and need adjustment along the way. Exhibit 3.2 suggests some questions to ask yourself as you develop your plans for goal achievement—and as the plans unfold. Returning to these questions can help you avoid getting stuck when things don't go as you hoped.

Just doing what you've planned to do is satisfying in itself, but it's also useful to build in rewards for completing tasks and accomplishing objectives. Rewarding yourself when you achieve a milestone can help keep your motivation and energy high when you hit the inevitable snags.

If you find a need to revise your goals, remember to ask yourself why. What went wrong? Did you have unrealistic expectations given your current skills? Did you set a schedule that no one could keep? Did obstacles get in your way? Or did you have the wrong goals to begin with? These questions will help you learn from the process—and avoid repeating any mistakes in the future. They will also help keep you flexible and able to adapt to changing circumstances. Such periods of reflection are essential to having a dream that still fits when you arrive.

Pay Attention to Feedback

Whether formal or informal, opportunities to assess how effectively you work with others are all around you. At work there's 360-

EXHIBIT 3.2. Questions to Ask When Planning to Meet Your Goals.

- What skills do I need to have to reach my goal?
- What knowledge or information do I need?
- Where do I need help?
- Who can help me?
- What other resources do I need?
- What resources do I have available; where do I need to seek or develop more?
- What are potential obstacles I might encounter?
- How might I avoid those obstacles?
- What are my strategies for coping with obstacles should they occur? Is there anything else I could do? Or anything I might do differently?
- Is this particular plan the only way to accomplish my goal?

degree feedback, and both at work and at home there's conversation that will reveal your impact on other people if you pay attention; often feedback in one realm is also relevant to the other. Feedback can help you assess how close you are to your goals. It can also let you know when you are getting off-track.

Walter Tornow, Manuel London, and CCL Associates (1998) suggest two ways feedback promotes effective agency. First, the disappearance of lifetime employment makes individuals responsible for managing their own performance, development, and careers. Feedback is an important tool for improving self-management and self-reliance, and you can incorporate feedback from others into your development plans and then gather more feedback along the way to monitor your progress. Listening actively to feedback can alert you to problems before they become disasters. And it may help you adapt in time to be ready for your future. By providing you with an assessment of your strengths and weaknesses, feedback empowers you to manage your future.

Second, these days enacting a role, carrying out a job, or completing an assignment often requires boundary-spanning activities and working in teams. Feedback can help you identify your critical constituencies so you can take a more active role in managing their demands. It can also help you identify tensions resulting from the multiple demands on your life and trade-offs that may help you balance more effectively. Feedback can also be a tool to help you build better working relationships, which may enhance agency as well by strengthening ties to others who are wiser or more powerful than you and who can provide you with resources, support, information, and opportunities to help you achieve your goals.

Remain Open to Possibilities

You now have a goal and a plan for getting there. But don't let yourself become so narrowly focused on your plan that you overlook or ignore opportunities that may come your way. One of the questions we asked women in our study was what advice they would give, what they had learned from their experiences that could be helpful to others. Many of them emphasized the need to be open to unexpected possibilities, using terms like these:

> Be willing to change directions. You never know where life is going to lead you. You may think you want to be an accountant, but hey, what if someone says, "Why don't you come work in marketing for a while?" Think about it. Be willing to change and be flexible about going in there and doing something different. Never look back and say "woulda, shoulda, coulda." Each thing is a new stepping-stone and it's a learning experience, and don't beat yourself up because maybe you made a wrong decision. Glean what you can learn from it and go on. With each move you make, think about what you want to accomplish. Be specific about what you want to learn, what skills you want to gain.

Empower Yourself

Most of all, to act effectively on your own behalf, you must believe in yourself. Have confidence and conviction in your plans—tempered with a healthy humility. You'll have many opportunities to feel challenged, discouraged, questioning, if not downright defeated. Every woman we spoke to expressed her own version of these feelings. Those who were most effective were able to find a measure of faith that the key to their getting out, surviving, and thriving lay within themselves. As one woman concluded:

> I'm a lot stronger than I thought I was. I've got to give myself a lot more credit probably than I have. I may not be able to control circumstances. Sometimes you simply cannot. But I can control the way I feel about things. And the way I act, my response to stress. And I can control myself enough to decide what things I will take on, and what things I'll just let pass through. So in that sense it doesn't feel like I'm out of control. The circumstance may be out of control, but I am not. Which is really a wonderful feeling, because in reality I think what's happened is through this situation, I've realized that I'm very much empowered. I've empowered myself.

Obstacles to Developing Greater Agency

Taking greater control over life rarely comes easily. Despite their success in their chosen fields, nearly all the women we interviewed had struggled for control at different times in their lives. They wanted to be agentic, but they did not want to sacrifice their relationships. When they did act agentically, they had to worry about how others would respond. In "A Modest Manifesto for Shattering the Glass Ceiling," Debra Meyerson and Joyce Fletcher (2000) suggest that gender inequity has not vanished, it has just gone underground. For example, they describe a company with a norm that managers would be available at any time to attend "emergency" meetings. This could create difficulties for anyone, of course, but it was particularly hard on women, who tend to have more demanding responsibilities outside work. Skipping a sudden meeting at an odd hour could mean missing out on important information. In these same meetings, managers often had to defend their turf. When men spoke up, they were seen as passionate and strong leaders, but when women did so, they were seen as overly controlling. Behavioral norms that differ in this fashion limit women's ability and willingness to take risks. This company isn't alone— many policies and practices that seem to apply equally to everyone actually have a differential impact on women and thus on their agency and effectiveness.

It isn't easy to balance assertive behavior with caring. Most women try to exert greater control, but many find that exercising the appropriate level of control means loosening up. They can develop what a few in our study described as an "overdeveloped sense of responsibility." This problem may result in part from the common feeling that women must work twice as hard as men to achieve the same result, and in part from the expectation that women will take care of others, thus taking responsibility for others' actions as well as their own. Stepping out in an agentic way meant seeking opinions of others and sharing more responsibility and information with staff members, being less rigid and controlling, and even learning to have more fun. They needed to avoid being overwhelmed by responsibilities at home and at work.

Gender stereotypes present a second obstacle for women attempting to become more agentic. According to a survey by the Conference Board of Canada (Griffith, MacBride-King, & Townsend, 1998), senior women managers see male stereotyping and men's preconceptions of women's roles and abilities as the top barrier to women's advancement. Although these women particularly identified stereotypes held by males, such stereotypes become ingrained in women as well. For an example of how stereotypes play out in the workplace, recall the 1980s Supreme Court case involving Price Waterhouse and Ann Hopkins. After working as a senior manager for four years, Hopkins became a candidate for partnership in 1984. When her application for partnership was denied, she filed suit against Price Waterhouse for alleged discrimination, since she had proven herself a hard-working, dedicated employee who had more billable hours than any other candidate. The firm claimed the primary reason for Hopkins's rejection was her perceived lack of "interpersonal skills" and her alleged mistreatment of staff. One partner criticized Hopkins for acting too "macho" while another claimed that she "overcompensated for being a woman." Yet another partner suggested that Hopkins lacked social graces and recommended that she "take a course at charm school," and the firm's Policy Board, after informing Hopkins of her rejection, recommended that she "walk more femininely, talk more femininely, dress more femininely, wear make-up, have her hair styled, and wear jewelry." The federal court ultimately ruled in favor of Ann Hopkins and awarded her $400,000 in compensatory damages. They found that the firm did discriminate against Ann Hopkins by permitting gender stereotypes to play a significant role in its decision to deny her a partnership. Hopkins had been in a no-win situation. If she came across as feminine she would be deemed unqualified for partnership because she was not aggressive enough. If she behaved as aggressively as her male colleagues she would be deemed unqualified because she was not feminine enough.

Besides the obstacles to agency posed by others, women often harbor obstacles of their own. Socialization can discourage women from attempting to act as agents on their own behalf, teaching them to emphasize relationships above individual achievement, and to derive feelings of power and reward from connections with other people rather than from competing and winning. Women raised in this pattern tend to believe the myth of meritocracy: if they just work hard and perform well, they will be rewarded. They take the "good things come to those who wait" approach. Unfortunately for them, although effort, skill, ability, and performance are indeed critical to career success, a number of less obvious factors also come into play. In a study of actual promotion decisions, we found that high-performing women who expected promotion often did not receive it until they lobbied for it (Ruderman & Ohlott, 1994). For example, one woman had been promised she would be promoted to the next level shortly after she accepted her position. When no promotion seemed to be forthcoming, she repeatedly asked her boss when it would happen. He kept telling her, "Soon." Finally, she sent him a memo with the dictionary definition of "soon." She was promoted shortly thereafter.

Several women acknowledged that they expected to be rewarded for good performance and that they would often wait and wait for their reward, their frustration and anger growing when recognition was not forthcoming. One remarked, "I would like a career path from my boss. I'd like a deliberate path. I'm reactive." Another who had just completed a project that involved many hundred-plus hour weeks confessed, "I realized that I do not do a good job selling myself. I guess I was expecting my boss to show a lot more appreciation for the dedication and more reward because I gave so much for the company. I essentially put everything else in my life on hold for this project. He gave the promotion I thought I deserved to someone else, a man, who had not proven himself as I had."

Male colleagues tended to be quicker to ask for, even demand, what they felt they deserved—and those who ask for rewards and promotions are likelier to get them than those who don't. In contrast, women often feel that assertiveness may lead them away from their connections with others, so they're reluctant to step out from among their peers. Because they tend to rely more on formal procedures and engage less in planning and managing their own careers, women may do better in organizations with strong career-management systems including tools such as prescribed career steps with clear criteria, or civil service–type exams.

If your organization does not take career planning seriously, you need to take matters into your own hands. Talk with your boss and other influential people. Let them know of your ambitions and seek their advice about steps toward achieving your goals. Volunteer for special projects and task force assignments to increase your visibility to key decision makers who can assist and support you. In one of our final interviews, a woman talked about working on building her confidence during the year: "I actually went and asked for this job. I could not have imagined myself doing that some time ago. I would have waited for the position to become available and for somebody else to say, 'Well, why don't you apply for that? You will be good at it.' I would have waited for them to approach me. I was too dependent on others for getting promotions."

Try interviewing a senior executive in your organization about what it takes to succeed there. Armed with this knowledge, you can begin to go after what you want. Prior to attending TWLP, participants were asked to complete such interviews. The responses they got varied widely across organizations and proved very helpful in figuring out what skills and abilities were most important to develop (as well as increasing their visibility to senior management!). Exhibit 3.3 provides an example of some questions you might ask in such an interview.

It can also be difficult to be agentic when things change and opportunities dry up. If your company reorganizes and the position you hoped for suddenly ceases to exist, what can you do to reach that goal? If your spouse loses his job or wants to do something different in his career, it may also affect your ability to achieve your own career goals. What do you do when life throws you such curveballs?

You may decide to wait and see if things improve—but don't wait too long or you will feel stuck. You may want to consider a detour—to find a different way to achieve the same goals. Or, after reevaluating your situation and your path, you may change your goal entirely and choose a new direction. Look for hidden possibilities, for benefits in the new situation; try to figure out ways you can influence what happens next. One woman who'd been particularly good at bouncing back after a series of personal and professional hardships shared her outlook with us: "I've learned never to think 'no' and never to take no for an answer. Always keep trying.

EXHIBIT 3.3. Senior Executive Interview.

Directions: The following questions provide structure for your interview, but you will want to ask follow-up and clarifying questions to make the discussion more valuable to you.

1. Taking into consideration the external environment and internal and organizational demands, what are the critical challenges you envision for this organization in the next three to five years?

2. Considering these challenges, what do you think are the required capabilities or perspectives to be effective in a leadership role? Could you give me an example that illustrates these capabilities? How does someone learn the things that are specific to our company?

3. What do you see as the key values that drive this organization? What is someone in a leadership position likely to be rewarded for here?

4. From your perspective what leadership issues do women face?

5. In terms of advancement, are there some factors that get in the way for women? What are those factors?

6. What are our organization's most challenging issues that women are prepared or not prepared to handle?

7. What are women's most challenging issues that our organization is prepared or not prepared to handle?

8. What are men's most challenging issues that our organization is prepared or not prepared to handle?

9. What are one or two critical lessons you have learned in the process of becoming an executive?

© Center for Creative Leadership

It's kind of like playing chess. I actually have a chessboard envisioned in my mind. The objects are different on a regular chessboard, but it's really the same. The strategy . . . you have to think about things and move things around. I call it 'wheeling and dealing' . . . it's a challenge and I enjoy it."

Inertia can also be an obstacle to agency. It is almost always easier not to challenge the status quo, to stay in a situation where you feel comfortable, even though it may not be the best thing for you. A new situation will involve new challenges and may call on capabilities you're not certain you possess, which can feel threatening. Changing your situation may also mean a disruption, a loss of equilibrium, and perhaps even a loss of control. One strategy some women used when contemplating an agentic step was to play the old "What's the worst that can happen?" game, asking themselves how bad things could get if they took this step—and if they did not take this step. Asking these questions can help you weigh the risks and benefits of potential actions and inactions. Robert Lee and Sara King (2001) suggest that managers who lead change need to integrate continuity with the change. Finding ways to maintain continuity in your values, goals, and sense of identity can help make it easier for you to take agentic steps in the face of uncertainty and stress. Try the following exercise:

Make a chart with five columns and three or four rows.

- Label the columns "Step I might take"; "Potential *positive* outcomes if I *do* this"; "Potential *negative* outcomes if I *do* this"; "Potential *positive* outcomes if I *do not* do this"; and "Potential *negative* outcomes if I *do not* do this."

- Number the remaining rows and label them with brief sketches of steps you're considering.

- Consider and list possible outcomes for each step in the appropriate column. You probably will not have an equal number of outcomes in every cell.

- Highlight the best and the worst possible outcomes for each potential step and compare them. Do the positives outweigh the negatives, or vice versa?

Simply listing, recognizing, and comparing the possible implications of action or inaction is an important first step toward agency. Based on this comparison, what will you choose to do next?

Clearly, agency is closely tied to the other four themes. It requires a degree of authenticity: to be effectively agentic you must understand yourself, what is important to you, and what you want out of work and life. You must be able to see whether you will be able to achieve your goals in the context of your current situation. You must also know yourself well enough to recognize whether you have the strengths necessary to achieve your goals and the time and other resources to help you get what you want. And you must avoid the pitfalls of unmitigated agency—if you burn your bridges to friends and associates, you will be less effective in reaching your goals as well as less happy with the end results.

4

Achieving Wholeness

Debbie's job keeps her working long hours seven days a week. Many old hobbies—tennis, camping, organizing group outings, theater, reading novels—have been crowded out, and she can no longer do anything just for fun. She used to exercise, but now work always takes precedence. Her bosses love her dedication to excellence and her diligence, but her subordinates experience her desire for perfection as unnecessarily demanding and controlling. At age forty, Debbie hasn't had a significant relationship in ten years, and she knows time is running out for having children. She doesn't have a close female friend, either, as her most recent promotion moved her to a distant district office. All her contact is with colleagues, most of whom are married men.

Debbie would like to pull back from work and develop other aspects of herself. Yet she worries that in doing so, she will lose her edge—and be left with a disappointing career as the center of her life. She is now a district manager, a long-sought goal, but she has just been passed over for a VP slot she had her eye on. With this disappointment, she is starting to suspect she has traded off too much of her personal life for her career. Debbie wonders if she can round out her life and still make VP the next time a slot opens. Although she acknowledges it's ungrounded, Debbie fears becoming a bag lady—washed up at the office and alone without family or friends.

Debbie is facing a critical life task. The desire to integrate life roles is a driving force in the behavior of many high-achieving women. It's the key issue for women today, according to Leonie Still (1993). The often onerous demands of the business world make integration hard to achieve. This problem manifests itself in two ways. Some high-achieving women, like Debbie, are so focused on their managerial role that they describe themselves as lopsided, lacking sources of satisfaction other than work. They earn huge salaries at the price of giving up almost everything apart from work. Others try to embrace identities outside work and end up feeling divided and torn. They see themselves as ripped into shreds as they try to satisfy the needs of their families, their jobs, and themselves. However, not every high-achieving woman goes through this struggle. We identified a group of women who did feel whole. They had coherent identities based on multiple roles in life, and felt well rounded, unified, and engaged.

Why Wholeness Matters

The managerial woman's desire for wholeness reflects a pervasive spiritual theme throughout human history. Across time and cultures, feeling whole has been recognized as central to well-being. Wholeness, the integration of all parts of the self into a sense of identity, is key to optimal human functioning: we need to feel whole to feel good about ourselves and to perform effectively over the long haul. Living a whole life allows us to address key psychological drives, and wholeness is related to well-being, a varied life rich in opportunities for learning, and a wide range of sources of social support.

Key Drives

Living a *whole life* allows a person to address human drives such as the need to be connected and the need to be agentic. Connection and agency were described in their own right in Chapters Two and

Three. Emphasizing one at the expense of the other leads to prob-lems. However, agency and connection need not exist in equal measure simultaneously, as long as the satisfaction of one drive does not preclude the possibility of addressing the other. Adults who address both drives satisfactorily feel more whole or complete. Actively engaging in multiple and varied life roles—caregiving, partnership, friendship, and community as well as occupation—makes it easier to attend to each drive. It pays to invest in roles in your personal life rather than just the managerial role at work.

Psychological Well-Being

Wholeness is related to psychological well-being (Bakan, 1966; Kaplan, Drath, & Kofodimos, 1991; Kofodimos, 1993). Numerous studies have demonstrated that both women and men who engage in multiple roles have higher levels of well-being than people who engage exclusively in one role in life (Barnett & Marshall, 1993; Crosby & Jaskar, 1993). In a 2001 literature review, Rosalind Bar-nett and Janet Hyde conclude that multiple roles are beneficial as reflected in a variety of indices of well-being. They suggest that people with a whole life feel better about themselves because a multiplicity of roles provides resources such as additional avenues of social support, buffering, and multiple opportunities for success.

If your life is overly focused on one role, the loss of that key role can be experienced as a total loss of meaning. It can result in a loss of gratification, identity, social networks, opportunities for learn-ing, and the like. Like Debbie at the start of this chapter, several women experienced the "bag lady fear"—without their jobs they would feel empty, unanchored, homeless, and disconnected.

With comments such as these, we were curious about the rela-tionship between wholeness and well-being in high-achieving women. We investigated the topic further with an additional group of 276 women who participated in TWLP. In this survey study (sum-marized briefly in the Appendix and described in full in Ruderman, Ohlott, Panzer, & King, 2002), we viewed wholeness as having a commitment to personal life roles beyond the managerial—partner, parenting, community, and friendship. We asked a series of questions evaluating commitment to these roles, from which we generated a global measure of commitment to roles outside work.

We found that higher commitment to personal life roles was associated with greater psychological well-being, measured in terms of general satisfaction with life and acceptance of self. This was true regardless of the woman's level of commitment to her management role, suggesting that someone who engages both personal and managerial roles has multiple ways to derive psychological well-being. Although we can't definitively prove that well-being is caused by having a whole life, these results suggest a strong connection. Think about your life. Do you feel the combination of activities in your personal life and your career make you feel better about yourself and happier with your life? Does a sense of variety in life contribute to your well-being?

Many women expounded on this phenomenon; they believed that well-being was related to a whole life, and they derived self-esteem from many types of activity: raising children, being a friend, being a wife, solving work problems, improving business results, contributing to the community. Their multiple sources of esteem were particularly helpful when trouble struck one aspect of life. For example, one woman going through a messy divorce took great comfort in successfully building a team at work. Another—caught in a lawsuit at work—was refreshed by helping her elderly father enjoy his retirement. A third, in the midst of a painful reorganization, found hope and satisfaction in her long and loving marriage. Consider this in your own life. Do both your personal and work roles contribute to your feelings of pleasure? Do they serve to validate your worth? Do they perhaps affirm complementary (or different) parts of yourself? These are ways a sense of wholeness contributes to well-being.

Another benefit was that having both sets of roles helped women bring perspective and objectivity to their problems. Several described outside roles as buffering the stress of work responsibilities.

Warm friendships and close family ties helped them turn off the tension of the workday and see that work is just an aspect of life— it's not life itself. Similarly, work provided solace to women experiencing personal stress.

The sense of psychological well-being associated with multiple roles is readily explained in scientific terms. Barbara Fredrickson, a University of Michigan psychologist, has found that positive emotions serve important functions in the development of well-being (2001). She has a "broaden-and-build" theory suggesting that positive emotions broaden people's mind-sets and build enduring psychological resources related to well-being. We take this to mean that having significant roles both inside and outside work offers additional venues for developing positive emotions that contribute to general psychological resources.

Enhanced Performance

It's not just a matter of feeling good, either—engagement in personal roles may also promote job performance, via a process called *role accumulation* (Marks, 1977; Sieber, 1974). This term means that learning from one role can be accumulated and incorporated into another. Thus, performance in one role can be enhanced by experience in another. Effectiveness in managerial jobs requires a wide range of skills—and different life experiences can develop the variety of skills modern managers need.

Managerial performance has two main components: capabilities to deal with people and capabilities to structure tasks (Stogdill & Coons, 1957). These have long been recognized as fundamental to the managerial role. Loosely speaking, dealing with people is a manifestation of connection and structuring tasks is a manifestation of agency. Personal life roles can offer experiences relevant to both these components.

Our survey study illuminated an association between multiple life roles and performance, both interpersonally and in terms of structuring tasks (Ruderman et al., 2002). We considered the same four personal roles as we did when looking at well-being—parent, partner, friend, and community volunteer—as they provide for a variety of experiences over and above the managerial role. We also had measures of managerial performance from observers in each woman's workplace—bosses, peers, and direct reports. We found that regardless of the level of commitment to the managerial role, the higher a manager's commitment to roles outside work, the higher her observers tended to rate her on both dimensions of performance. It's worth repeating: *commitment to private life roles is associated with high performance in the more public sphere of work.*

Again, we cannot prove that multiple roles cause increased job performance for women; all we can say is that they are linked. But the association is striking. If the assumption that women have to sacrifice everything for their careers is correct, why would we find that as women commit to roles outside work, performance ratings increase? This finding suggests that different facets of life inform and enrich each other, challenging the conventional assumption that the best employees prioritize work above all else. It also suggests that women can and should integrate various life roles, bringing skills from one realm into another. All work and no play makes for a dull manager.

Opportunities to Transfer Learning

It's simple, when you think of it: more life roles create more opportunities to learn skills and behaviors relevant to management. Each role teaches many lessons, and the lessons learned in one domain often transfer to another. We asked how the experiences women had in their personal lives contributed to their managerial performance. (We also asked how their managerial role contributed to their personal lives. Although that is not our focus here, skills and self-confidence learned on the job did carry over to the personal sphere.) Personal roles enhanced managerial performance in four main areas: relational skills, multitasking skills, using personal background to understand constituents, and leadership practice.

Relational Skills. The women reported that they learned how to understand, motivate, and respect others through their personal life and were then able to carry those abilities over into their roles at work. Parenting was particularly useful in this area; these high-achieving women reported many managerial lessons from the experience of being a mother. They learned patience, respect for individual differences, motivation techniques, how to develop others, influence skills, acceptance of failure, empathy, and how to give feedback. Virtually every mother interviewed in the study mentioned learning something managerially relevant from mothering.

In addition to parenting, the women also cited learning relational skills from other family relationships, friendships, and community relationships. One, for example, explained that she learned how to deal with difficult people at work by dealing with difficult people at home. She said, "If I can get along with my mother-in-law and brother-in-law, I can get along with anyone at work." In-law relations can be a proving ground for getting along with people with whom you share an important interdependency.

Volunteering in the community also taught valuable lessons. One woman gained coaching skills as a lay counselor at her church. She said, "At work I can apply the same listening skills, questioning skills, and communication skills, which gives me a broader dimension than what other people bring to the manager role." She felt she was a much better coach to her staff after she established herself in the church-counseling role than before.

The reports of learning relational skills from private roles in the family and community are significant. These skills, which are manifestations of emotional intelligence, are now seen as essential in organizations. Daniel Goleman (1998) argues that these skills are critical to good performance. But where are these skills learned? Joyce Fletcher (1999) argues that organizations don't discuss where relational skills are developed. She suggests that these skills can be learned in the private sphere through active roles in caregiving and volunteer work, and the reports of the women in this study support her hypothesis.

Multitasking.   Planning and prioritizing multiple tasks at home are good practice for juggling multiple managerial responsibilities. Taking care of children, a house, a job, and a spouse promotes efficiency, focus, and organization. Dealing with and strategizing about family issues such as elder care and child care helped women we spoke with build their abilities to develop complex arrangements and anticipate problems.

Personal Interests and Background.   Personal interests and background also contributed to work performance. For example, one well-traveled executive explained how living in different countries in her youth improved her handling of global responsibilities at the executive level. The daughter of a diplomat, she had developed both skills and interest in getting to know people in different cultures as the family moved. She was able to use these skills to the company's benefit on the job. In addition, the travel component of her job gave her a chance to do something she really enjoyed that kept her motivated and challenged. In a similar way, women used their personal consumer experience to influence their business decisions:

> Jennifer said, "I am a consumer and I happen to work for a company that sells products that the gatekeeper for, if you will, is me. I may not be typical because of income and position in my job, but the female that shops the supermarket or shops for the family is typically going to be twenties to forties. . . . If you're looking to appeal to the gatekeeper, to the decision maker in the household, you're looking to appeal to people that think kind of like me." Jennifer used her personal role as a grocery shopper for a family of four to influence her marketing approach at work, where she was the only one on the strategy team who had primary responsibility for family grocery shopping.

Leadership.   Volunteer positions provide a great way to practice leadership responsibilities. Some of the women told us that leadership roles in their personal lives helped them at work: leadership in family businesses and in community and religious organizations improved their leadership skills on the job.

As a homemaker, Karen had been curious what life would be like as a manager. To get a taste, she ran for president in a local women's organization. She found she really liked being involved, setting direction, working to bring together a team and implement a vision. She reasoned that if she could motivate people to work for free, surely she could do so for a paycheck—so she tried her hand in work outside the home. Karen found that the skills she developed as a volunteer were an important asset on the job.

Take a moment to review your own life. Think about skills you've developed outside work that could enhance your managerial performance. Write down your personal life roles. What are you learning from them? Can any of these competencies be translated into job-related skills? Can any of your personal life roles help you develop new skills needed on the job?

Support from Others

A final reason that a whole life is important is that such a life offers multiple sources of support and comfort. This is a recurrent finding in the literature on management and executive development. Managerial work by its very nature is extremely demanding and fraught with stress, and support from other people can help buffer or soften its challenges. Managers who were actively engaged in multiple roles had ready sources of support for dealing with difficulties at work. They had family and friends to help them figure out how to deal with work-related problems. They also had people at work to help them when personal-life issues seemed overwhelming. They had people to distract them from difficult situations. They had relationships in other parts of their lives to sustain them when they experienced painful changes at work or at home.

Think about your own network of support. Who helps you buffer the stresses of life? Who helps you to get perspective on problems at work? At home?

Problems of Wholeness for High-Achieving Women

Many women described craving a sense of wholeness in their lives. In theory, they can address their needs for agency and connection in ways that were unavailable to earlier generations of women. Through their work roles, they can change their environment, make things happen, and act independently and get results. Through their family and friendship roles they can nurture others and help others achieve their own goals. The reality, however, is that organizations really want managers to emphasize agentic behavior. As Joan Kofodimos (1993) notes in her study of executive men, Western culture has norms and values that contribute significantly to the focus on work behavior. With the emphasis on results, accomplishments, and achievements, there is little encouragement to spend time satisfying needs for connectedness in other than a cursory way. This led to two types of problems of wholeness for the women in our study: problems of putting everything into work and problems of trying to combine work with outside interests.

Workaholism

Those who described themselves as workaholics—like Debbie at the start of this chapter—had major difficulties feeling whole. Although long recognized as a problem for men, workaholism is relatively new among women. Its victims resemble the male executives Robert Kaplan and his colleagues (1991) described as "expansive"—achievement oriented, results focused, and hard driving. They emphasize agentic behavior so much that they have little time to address their needs for connection, and they devote themselves to work, gathering all their self-esteem through their work life. They told us stories of working seventy-hour weeks, handling multiple assignments at the same time, being too busy to take vacations. For a woman living this way, her career is her life. Status and recognition matter so much that she doesn't allow room for anything or anyone else. She is obsessed with work. In *When Work Doesn't Work Anymore* (1997), Elizabeth Pearle McKenna described such women as having a "business card identity." They see themselves purely in professional terms.

Because their self-esteem is tied up in their work, they can be very demanding and difficult to work with. Such women see any minor lapse on the part of someone working for them as a reflection on their own abilities, and therefore it becomes a major issue. Those who fit this pattern were described by their subordinates as excessively controlling.

Workaholic managers tend to be happy for a while with a life consumed by career. Eventually, something happens at work that makes them want to broaden their lives. Often, as with Debbie, this pivotal event involves missing a promotion. Work loses its savor and they feel lopsided and out of balance, realizing they have put so much energy into work life that there's little left over for anything else. Women like Debbie wonder what happened to their personal identity. Hard work has eroded their lives to a point where they fear they have nothing but their career. They begin to feel they can't enjoy life. They feel way out of control. These women recognize that their life structure no longer serves all their needs and they want a different type of life that does not require the sacrifice of key aspects of themselves.

Regina is another striking example of this phenomenon. Brilliant, capable, and talented, Regina has excelled all her life. She was valedictorian of her high school class, Phi Beta Kappa in college, and a star at Harvard Business School. She devoted all her energies to her career with little time for friends or hobbies. She spent holidays with her older brother and his family, but other than that took little time for celebration or fun. Everything was going well with her career in a Fortune 50 company until her boss left and her division was reorganized. Regina was offered a significant position leading a marketing initiative into the former Soviet Union for a new line of business. It would require moving to St. Petersburg with extensive travel in Russia.

Taking the job would foster her career—but what about her personal life? As an American woman in Russia, she would have a very lonely time, with little opportunity for intimacy. At age forty, Regina hopes to one day marry or have a significant relationship. She also wants to be CEO of a major company but is starting to wonder about the level of personal sacrifice required. Making over $250,000 a year, Regina wondered, "What is all the success for if I don't have anyone to share it with? What is the point of having all this money if I don't have people to whom to leave it behind? What else is there?" Regina felt dissatisfied and sought to realign her life. She spoke eloquently about wanting to feel whole and complete. She realized that success in life meant more than material things such as how much money you make, your status, and your job title. Over the course of a year, Regina worked to redefine success for herself, moving slowly from her previous material focus to include connection with others. She actively sought to develop aspects of herself besides the achiever and made a conscious choice to spend time cultivating friends and connecting with family. This included taking on a new job in a different organization with less of a workaholic culture. It was the first time she had ever allowed herself to be in anything but a high-pressure situation. Regina also joined a golfing club and made a commitment to spend weekly time with her brother and his family.

A subgroup of women like Regina were so work-oriented that they neglected their health. Not only did they subordinate their need for connection to their need for agency but they also forgot to nurture themselves. This could be easily overlooked when they were healthy, but it became harder when medical conditions entered the picture. Many were diagnosed with chronic illnesses that could be ameliorated with a less stressful lifestyle—but they felt unable to follow the medical advice because work always beckoned. They had problems like back pain, ulcers, colitis, and asthma.

Eventually some of them were stopped in their tracks by physical pain or symptoms so severe they could not get out of bed. That is the point when many women discover they have no one to take care of them. Regina was diagnosed with a serious chronic illness that caused her to reconsider her priorities. Her brother was her only confidant. Busy with his own life, he was unable to provide the support she suddenly needed. Her pervasive aloneness once masked by her work schedule became brutally obvious.

Work-Life Conflicts

A second way issues of wholeness arose was through conflict between work and personal life. This issue has gotten much attention in the media. Women intent on satisfying their drives for both agency and connection want to do it all, but addressing that desire comes at a cost. A study of women managers in Canada (Beatty, 1996) found that feelings of conflict between work and family were related to anxiety, depression, and hostility.

Work and personal roles create competing demands in terms of time and energy. Women live in two different worlds and they fear failing in both. Often they feel the different pieces of their lives are at war with one another. They worry that there is something wrong with them.

> Tina was the only woman in a group of men, most of whom had stay-at-home wives. She worked fifty-five to sixty hours a week trying to prove herself, but it was a losing battle. Her boss didn't trust her or take her seriously because she had two children and a third on the way, and he bought into the stereotype that a woman with children is an uncommitted employee. Although she never lost time for a sick child (her mother stepped in when the children needed home care), she knew her boss was just waiting for it to happen. The decision to have a second child was the nail in her coffin at work. With the announcement of her third, she began to feel she would never get ahead. No matter how hard she tried, her male coworkers saw her as less than serious

about her job. Despite this, she had been with the company for many years and had risen rapidly there. The group she managed was highly productive despite the environment.

Every day, Tina wondered about her kids. Was she spending enough time with them? The little one was developing more slowly than his sister. Was it because Tina wasn't there? She felt tense and stressed, and never felt there was enough time to do anything well. Sometimes she wondered if she should quit. Tina began to feel her identity as a mother was incompatible with her company's expectations for a manager.

Eventually, much to Tina's relief, her boss was fired for incompetence that went beyond mishandling Tina's career. The tension lessened in the more comfortable work environment that resulted, but it did not go away. Tina still struggled with the pull between wanting to give sixty or more hours a week to her job and wanting to be available to her children every minute they were at home and awake.

Unfortunately, Tina's situation is all too typical. Many women want it all and struggle with how to get it in the face of an inflexible environment. And many bosses who make life difficult remain on the job year after year, so most women can't look forward even to Tina's partial escape.

What Does Wholeness Look Like?

Although wholeness is difficult to achieve, it is not impossible. We spoke to managerial women of all ages who did feel whole. These women tended to understand their own identity and their various needs and responsibilities. They fashioned a life that put them in environments where they could fulfill a wide variety of needs and feel both agentic and connected. Some emphasized agency more than connection, others put connection ahead of agency. No one form of balance was perfect. What was common to all who felt whole was that they addressed both types of goals through an array of roles.

The woman who feels whole has a sense of self based on multiple facets. She views herself as having many identities—manager, negotiator, spouse, confidante, mother, implementer, nurturer. She is able to weave these pieces together in a coherent way. In most cases, feelings of wholeness were not reached easily; they were often achieved after much soul-searching and active restructuring of life to identify and integrate priorities.

Consider the case of Amanda, a forty-six-year-old manager. Amanda stood out as a good example of someone who has achieved wholeness.

Through her roles as business manager, spouse, daughter, friend, and homemaker she was able to fulfill her needs for both agency and connection. Her peers described her as a respected natural leader who cared about others. She excels at developing strategies and implementing them. Amanda eloquently described her view of life:

> *Every day holds a glass full of liquid that has something spiritual in it, that has something with my husband in it—we have a dog, so it has it in it, and it has work in it, and they're woven together. Maybe one day it's all clients or 90 percent clients and 10 percent family and whatever. Maybe another day is something else. It's not so much that it is balanced but it's more that there's richness because you have so many different parts of yourself operating. I don't think I would have said this five years ago but for me, it's really about weaving all the threads of one's life together in a coherent way.*

Amanda goes on to say that her professional and personal lives are intertwined, which contributes to a feeling of coherence. For example, she finds that her personal hobbies, reading and singing, make her more appealing to clients. An internal management consultant, her clients enjoy her because she has such a broad range of interests. Success at work helps buffer the sadness she feels about her mother's declining health. Amanda and her husband review their work with one another and give each other suggestions. She describes themselves as "co-advisors." They also view themselves as co-leaders of the household. When work starts to take up too much time, Amanda purposely builds in other activities like cultivating new friendships and taking art classes. When there is a business crunch, she makes a concerted effort not to let it stop her life. In fact the day before a major presentation, she entertained and had enormous fun even though her natural proclivity would have been to be considerably stressed. The next day, she felt the presentation to clients went well because she was relaxed, calm, and patient. Amanda's philosophy is to combine and interweave things in her life. Her personal life relaxes her and gives her the perspective she needs to deal with her work.

Elise was another person who valued wholeness and lived her life in a way that made her feel total and complete.

Elise, a forty-year-old executive at a major international company, has two young children, one with a chronic health problem. Although she says that maintaining a feeling of wholeness is a constant struggle, she has a very good handle on it. She has been with the same company for her entire career. She is now on the operating committee, which reports to the president, and has total responsibility for two businesses. Her job has significant bottom-line responsibility and a huge head count.

Earlier in her life, Elise was a real workaholic. Her younger daughter's illness forced her to take a look at how she was living her life. She started counseling, and one of the things she learned was that doing things with her kids helped to take her away from the craziness at work. She spends a lot of time now with her children. Elise also decided to focus on interests that give her energy. She realized that she is very interested in women's issues and took this on as part of her identity. This passion influenced her decision to coach her elder daughter's soccer team. She also started a women's networking group in her predominantly male company, and has found she can use some of the coaching skills she is developing from the women's network with her daughter's teammates. Likewise, coaching the youngsters has helped to improve her patience at work. Through both opportunities she has made friends for herself with other women with the same passion. She feels she is making a difference in the world. Elise gets a lot of satisfaction from advocating for women in two very different environments.

At the moment, Elise knows her priorities very well and sets boundaries accordingly. She guards her time very carefully. At work, once she gets an initiative started, she has learned how to step back and let others take over. Elise sees delegation as a way to set boundaries and protect her time. She also puts a lot of emphasis on scheduling, including scheduling time for herself to exercise and simply relax. On the home front, too, she delegates and schedules, giving homecare tasks to a nanny and carving out time for herself. She and her husband negotiate how to spend their weekends to make the most of their time together.

Elise also says that she has given up on perfection and control. She has learned to accept that she can't micromanage everything and still have a full life. She is now confident accepting the work of others. She doesn't feel she has to do everything herself or that it has to be done her way. This was hard at first. Being the first woman at her level in the organization, Elise felt she couldn't afford to fail. However, she realized trusting others and sharing control was the only way to succeed both at work and personally. At home she has learned to accept the way the nanny and her husband do things even if it's different from the way she would do them herself. She realized that letting others assume responsibility is a way to have both an involved workforce and a healthy family life. She has also realized that she can't do everything she wants to, but feels that she can accomplish her most important goals, raising physically and emotionally healthy children while growing a business.

Letting go of the ideal of perfection often seems to be key to success in feeling whole. Sharing power allows a woman to delegate, which frees her up to do what is most important.

How Can You Achieve a Sense of Wholeness?

Developing wholeness is not a simple activity learned in a few days or hours. It is a complex process that takes place over time and never really ends, as wholeness requires active maintenance—you can't take it for granted. Based on the experience of women who developed wholeness in their lives, this section describes five techniques that you can use to build a sense of coherence and wholeness in your own life. (See Exhibit 4.1.) Not every technique will be effective for everyone. As you read through these, think about what strategy will work best with your life.

EXHIBIT 4.1. A Developmental Thumbnail for Understanding and Achieving Feelings of Wholeness.

1. Establish clear priorities.

2. Set boundaries.
   - Schedule
   - Delegate
   - Share responsibilities
   - Say no

3. Incorporate time for reflection and spirituality.
   - Meditation
   - Yoga
   - Inspirational reading
   - Journaling
   - Religious practices

4. View yourself holistically.

5. Restructure your thoughts.
   - Review your thoughts on being a perfectionist.
   - Enjoy the here and now.
   - Keep at it! Reassess and redesign your life structure as conditions change.

Establish Clear Priorities

This is the most basic technique for increasing feelings of wholeness. The women who felt whole were very clear on their priorities. They lived by their values. It is important to know what you really want. A structured life always requires giving up something, and without knowing your own values you can't feel whole—you're never sure that you have chosen to keep what really matters to you. That means you must understand what you cannot give up, what you can do without, and what you feel must be added.

For some women, this self-knowledge comes very easily, for others it is more of a struggle.

Nancy, one of our participants with the most years of education, took a new job three thousand miles away from her young son. This job was her dream job—the gold standard in her profession and the one she fantasized about all through graduate school. She thought she could take it on and mother her son, already living with his father, long distance. But the reality was different. It was too hard to go through the weeks without seeing her son. It was too hard to manage the three-hour time difference that limited when and where she could call her son. Although the job provided her with a unique opportunity that she really wanted, Nancy was heartbroken about the lack of contact with her son. It took painful soul-searching for her to realize that she did not want this great job at the expense of missing her child. Even though her son had been primarily living with his father prior to her move, she had been playing a daily role in his life when they were in the same city. Nancy felt like a loser when she thought about giving up the position her mentors and advisers had encouraged her to take. She ended up leaving the job. Once she understood her priorities, she was better able to deal with her feelings and a course of action became clear. She could get another job, albeit less prestigious and with a different employer, that allowed her to be closer to her son. The new job still allowed her to feed her soul intellectually, provided income, and had opportunities for advancement. Most important, it would let Nancy satisfy both the need to work and the need to mother. The clarity on her priorities, in particular what she could not do without, helped her to take action. She realized she had to be true to her values and her needs.

Remember that priorities need to be rebalanced periodically. As women reviewed their life stories, we realized that those who felt whole had reassessed their priorities during their career and—like Elise—realigned life accordingly. They saw life as a series of choices with periodic opportunities to review relative priorities over time. They changed their ordering as opportunities presented themselves and as they and their children aged. At different junctures they compromised different needs and desires. They kept in mind the idea that any single decision forms just one chapter of life; it is not the whole story.

Set Boundaries

Be a strong scheduler and preserve your private time. Once you understand what is most important to you, then you can work to protect the time and energy you choose to commit to those roles or activities. Many women in our study wanted more time with family and to connect with friends, or more time alone to pursue nonwork interests. They found the additional time and energy by setting boundaries or limits around their work life. Some set limits regarding the people they dealt with and the problems they tackled. For example, one looked through her portfolio of job functions and determined that she would completely delegate certain responsibilities. Another handed off a set of routine problems to a subordinate. A third asked a key subordinate to act as a liaison for her with certain groups of people. Others set limits on their schedules. Many who traveled for their work set limits on the number and length of trips.

Women who felt whole also set boundaries around their personal lives. They reviewed what they wanted to do personally and figured out how to protect those activities. They hired nannies, cleaning services, and errand-running services so as to be able to spend their nonwork time the way they desired. They enlisted their husbands (and ex-husbands) in child rearing—not something they viewed as getting help from a spouse but as *sharing* parenting. In essence the women set boundaries around their different roles so they could address all their priorities.

By learning how to say no and mean it they learned to protect time for their top priorities. They took steps to ensure their time was spent on the activities of greatest importance to them. An excellent resource on how to redesign your work to allow for outside roles is the Third Path Institute, at http://www.thirdpath.org/. This institute talks about approaches to redesigning work in order to have more time for parenting, but you can use similar methods to create time for other personal roles.

Incorporate Time for Reflection and Spirituality

To increase feelings of wholeness, many of the most effective women took the time to stop and reflect on their lives. This was particularly helpful for those who felt torn between work and family. Adding spirituality helped to enhance wholeness by creating feelings of centeredness and perspective. Spirituality can come in many forms—meditation, yoga, inspirational reading, organized religion, silent prayer. Reflection wasn't always easy to do, but when women who were extremely stressed by the competing demands of significant roles took time for it they greatly benefited. Pausing for reflection was a great source of comfort to women in the throes of simultaneous life emergencies.

View Yourself Holistically

Many women who felt whole were able to see themselves in a unified way, transcending their different roles. They had flow and coherence because they integrated their self-concept. Elise's focus on herself as a developer of women is a good example of this approach. It guided her selection of personal involvements as well as her choice of initiatives to sponsor at work. Another woman held a strategic planning role at work and let this identity carry over into private life—strategic planning smoothed her way through family activities (such as arranging child care, making summer plans, giving parties, setting family financial goals, and designing elder care plans) and community roles (chairing the long-range planning committee at her children's school).

It is important to note that those who felt whole did not try to be all things to all people. Rather, they knew their most important needs and desires and saw that they had ample opportunity to satisfy them. Being whole doesn't mean that these women didn't spend a lot of time at work. Rather, it means that the women experienced the different parts of themselves as actively integrated in a way that was unified and coherent. One way to develop this view is to ask yourself if there is any unifying theme in your life. Identify the qualities in yourself that you feel best define you and see if those qualities can help you to develop an overarching identity.

Restructure Your Thoughts

Are you ruminating about how torn and divided you feel? Do you feel tense because you feel you have so much to do that you aren't doing anything well? If so, consider changing the way you think about your life so that the tension between different roles isn't so debilitating. Some of the women in the study let go of their desire for perfection, as Elise did before she could feel complete. Letting go of perfectionist standards didn't happen overnight. Women worked on it for months or even years. They decided that they didn't have to be the perfect manager, wife, and mother and that it was okay to simply be a good manager, wife, and mother. Some said they learned to let go of the standards of housecleaning their mother had set and gave themselves permission to have a messy house— feeling vast relief when they realized nothing bad happens if the beds aren't made every day. As they changed their thinking the tension between different life roles reduced. This is something that is difficult to do on your own. Virtually all the women who changed their assessments of their life participated in professional counseling or had a career coach. The counseling helped them change their perceptions so as to reduce the stress of trying to deal with their many roles. In addition to the counseling and in a few cases in place of it, they had a lot of support from friends and family for letting go of excessive standards. They used a variety of techniques for reducing the pressure they put on themselves to do everything well. The women forgave themselves for not being perfect and realized that doing one's best under the circumstances is good enough.

Another cognitive restructuring technique useful for increasing feelings of wholeness is to focus on one thing at a time, and savor your moments of pleasure and delight. Enjoy what you are doing without letting worries about other responsibilities interfere. Live in the here and now. This, too, is easier said than done. However, several of the women who sought wholeness managed it. They learned to think about time with their children and enjoy the interaction rather than ruminating about a political conflict at work. They learned to enjoy finishing a report rather than worrying about a husband's new job. The key is to fully involve yourself in the situation you are in at the moment without being distracted by other responsibilities. This can be learned through concentration and effort. In trying to make this type of cognitive restructuring it is helpful to get support from others who say, "It's okay." Identify for yourself a set of support people to help you restructure your thoughts.

Obstacles Faced on the Journey to Wholeness

Many obstacles interfere with increasing one's wholeness. The most prominent is the organizational environment; most organizations simply don't care if their managers feel whole. In fact, organizations embody an implicit belief that workaholic cultures promote the organizational interest. They encourage a lopsided view of life that makes work paramount. Career ladders are designed to reward people who prioritize work above other roles. It is very difficult to move toward wholeness when you are in an environment that encourages the opposite. In the face of the strength of this norm, the women who worked on wholeness had a tough time sticking to the goal. Many set limits and then slipped back. The key to overcoming this obstacle was to consciously work on the wholeness issue. To that end, taking time for reflection or developing oneself spiritually helped to keep the wholeness goal in the forefront. This seemed to help combat the organizational push for results, results, and more results.

As noted earlier, organizations face a paradox here. Complete dedication seems so desirable that they set up systems to promote total devotion to the workplace, but commitment to non-work roles is actually associated with greater performance. Organizations would be better off allowing managers to develop, maintain, and enrich outside interests. We contend that organizations that sustain a climate encouraging wholeness will reap rich rewards in terms of performance. Organizations would be better off with policies, practices, and cultures that support managers' involvement in life outside of work. Artificially precluding such involvements limits individual well-being and performance.

Organizations don't pose the only obstacle to wholeness. Norms for the roles and responsibilities of women are at fault as well, continuing to suggest that women should do it all. According to society, real women should be full-time mothers totally devoted to their children and husbands. Many of the women in our study internalized the TV model of the conventional family and thus had the cookie-baking mommy embedded in their mental image of a good woman. These societal ideals are hard to fulfill when you are working forty to sixty hours a week. Trying to do so can be a recipe for disaster. Many high-achieving women feel guilty going against the image of the ideal mother, who is always available. Consciously understanding your priorities and how they may differ from society's is the only way to deal with this internal conflict.

The women who felt whole also felt free to depart from expectations that ran counter to their own values and priorities. This was never easy, but support from counselors, friends, family, and colleagues helped. Those who felt whole created their own visions of the ideal worker, the ideal mother, and the ideal woman.

Working on wholeness is a challenge for women in this day and age. Organizations expect complete devotion, especially on the part of women and people of color who are trying to prove themselves in corporate America. Society says it is okay for women to enter the business world as long as they don't fall down on the job of taking care of children, home, hearth, and elders. Developing your sense of wholeness in this context requires a strong understanding of your priorities and the will to live by them even if others place obstacles in your way. Wholeness was the most common area for developmental growth chosen by the women in our study. And despite its exceptional difficulty, many of them made great strides in their quest for wholeness during the year we knew them.

5

Gaining Self-Clarity

Self-clarity is knowing who you are and how you fit into the world—how forces built into your organization and your larger society affect the way others see you. It also means developing a view of yourself that reflects your preferences, priorities, strengths, and weaknesses. A strong sense of self-clarity enables you to navigate effectively through life.

Self-clarity is a fundamental human desire and one that acts as a facilitator for growth in the four other themes. It allows you to recognize your values so as to live authentically, enables agentic behavior, improves your ability to connect with others, and allows you to make choices that produce feelings of wholeness.

Self-clarity goes beyond self-awareness, which involves accurate understanding of your own strengths and weaknesses. Women with self-clarity are not just self-aware, they incorporate their own self-view into a realistic assessment of the world and what it means for them. They take a long-term perspective and can describe patterns in their lives over time with insight and wisdom. They understand their desires relative to the norms of the organization and society in general. This insight allows them to make conscious choices about life. They have a certain objectivity about themselves in relationship to others and they understand how others have shaped them. Women high in self-clarity approach transitions and chaotic situations with the perspective that they can learn something from them regardless of what happens, and they can admit mistakes and learn from failures as well as successes. Self-clarity allows them to address problems and reframe courses of action.

Why Self-Clarity Matters

Self-clarity provides a map that can keep you on course and lead to a fulfilling professional and personal journey. It not only pinpoints where you are, it describes the terrain around you. It helps you to navigate through the many choices and obstacles you face as a woman manager.

First, self-clarity helps you figure out what you want and what your gifts and talents are. Then it shows you your surroundings, what your relationship to your world is and where you might go in it—it puts a "You are here" marker on your personal map. Without a basic level of self-clarity, you are in danger of accepting situations that don't match your core preferences and needs. On the work front, self-clarity helps you find a job in line with your talents, one that lets you build on your strengths and satisfy your desires for meaningful and enjoyable work.

Nora is frustrated and bored. She chose corporate communications because she likes to write—but what she likes to write is fiction. Although her job involves more elements of fiction than her managers would care to acknowledge, more often than not it requires writing about business policy, technical issues, and corporate performance in the most prosaic terms. Nora sees herself as a free spirit in a rather straitlaced environment, and her performance is shaky—she is not preparing materials consistent with the CEO's directives. Yet she went into the job fully aware that it would call for a type of writing she disdained in a company with a well-known conservative bent.

In choosing this job, Nora took her strengths into account but not her preferences, and she is swimming upstream as a result. She would be much better off now if she had considered her preferred working environment as well as her writing talents before signing on.

This isn't the first time this has happened to Nora. She can't seem to find the right career path because she misjudges what she needs. Her many attempts—sometimes in the same company, sometimes by changing companies—can only be approximations to a better fit since she is not wholly clear about what she would most like.

Compare Nora to Ellie.

Ellie got her MBA with a specialization in finance. She then went to work in an investment banking firm as a stock analyst. She learned quickly that this choice didn't suit her creative, free spirit even though it paid well and she was successful. Deciding she couldn't deny her true self for the sake of compensation and prestige, she left the investment banking firm and went to work for an art auction house, where she could be herself (that is, "wear her green suede boots to work" and be comfortable with the people and the conversation) and still make use of her finance skills. Ellie finds that this artsy environment is just right for her—she knew herself well enough to realize how to improve her fit with her job.

A second reason self-clarity matters is that it helps you deal with the demands of modern adult life. In *In Over Our Heads*, Robert Kegan (1994) describes the adult maturation process as learning to see oneself as clearly and objectively as possible. The better you understand yourself in relationship to others and to the context you are embedded in, the better you can deal with partnering, parenting, and working. Effective maturation rests on a clear sense of self in context.

A third reason self-clarity is important is that it can help you perform better as a manager, allowing you to identify performance obstacles before they occur or as they occur so you can address them. Further, a clear self-view can help you create a developmental plan to enhance your strengths and shore up your managerial weaknesses. Without a sense of how you are affecting others, it is difficult to take the steps necessary to improve.

The self-awareness aspect of self-clarity has been linked with effective managerial performance for both men and women. Church

(1997) demonstrated a clear link between self-awareness and performance on the job, as perceived and rated by colleagues in terms of behavior on several managerial competencies. Understanding yourself improves your response both to the environment and to the people around you, and it helps you see the best way to make your contribution. Self-clarity helps you sort out the reasons for complex events by knowing yourself well, knowing your environment well, and not confusing the two.

A fourth reason self-clarity is important has to do with the gendered nature of organizations. As noted earlier, organizations tend to be tailored to meet old-fashioned ideas of masculinity. Modern organizations were built by and for men. Identifying their masculine norms and understanding one's own relationship to them is crucial for women. Self-clarity is a big help here, allowing you to see how organizational gender expectations influence your private experience. Once you understand that linkage, you can tell when to push back on the organization, when to accommodate it, when to ignore it, and when to leave it.

Working for Self-Clarity

Managerial women constantly struggle with the development of self-clarity. Perfect self-clarity is neither a state you can expect to achieve nor a skill you can learn and keep without further thought. Like the other themes in this book, it is a condition that you strive for and work at, adjusting as conditions change. The more self-clarity you have, the more you feel its benefits and the more likely you are to strive for continued development. Conversely, the less you have, the less likely you are to recognize the need to work on it—or even see it as something to strive for.

Issues of Low Self-Clarity

Careening into an Obstacle. The most noticeable characteristic of women low in self-clarity is that they tend to run into obstacles stemming from their own needs, weaknesses, or limitations without seeing the problem coming or making any attempt to slow down or brace themselves for the impact. Life poses stumbling blocks for everyone, but many people can spot them a ways off and choose to evade them or at least ask someone for help or brace themselves for the impact. Women low in self-clarity never even see the obstacle until they run into it, head first. Even then they are not sure what happened because they thought they had done everything right. It is hard for them to correct their behavior because they don't see that they made any errors. They claim the obstacle wasn't their fault—somebody else put it in their path—rather like the driver whose accident report claimed a tree ran into the front of the car. These career stumbling blocks take different forms—but every woman we saw as low in self-clarity had run into at least one.

> Laurie worked in a research laboratory where her teammates and her boss were hard workers who all kept to themselves and preferred quiet evenings at home to office parties and never felt like a quick drink after work to wind down. Department meetings tended to be brisk, operating by the principle of "Why say it in a paragraph when a sentence will do?" Notices of key issues were sent by e-mail prior to meetings so that people could think about them beforehand and make their contributions as quickly as possible. But Laurie craved a more sociable atmosphere. She tended to report in full on the progress of each project, not just give a brief précis of its current state. She liked to discuss problems in a group and didn't relish thinking about them alone in her office. Every time she came across an interesting problem she phoned her boss to share it. She kept trying to win him over by giving him detail, stopping by his office with stories, and asking him about his personal life. Her boss—who liked being an introvert among introverts—saw these efforts as intrusive. Moreover, he believed Laurie didn't think before she spoke. The others on the team thought she talked way too much. Needless to say, Laurie did not thrive in this environment.

Laurie and her boss had opposite personality types. He was a classic introvert and she was a classic extrovert. But Laurie kept trying the same moves over and over again and never thought of adjusting her tactics. Her career didn't progress at the lab—and she never realized why.

> For Francesca, the career stumbling block was her blindness to changing market conditions. Despite a soft overall market that led others on the team to sense trouble brewing, Francesca led her team as she always had. Some of her peers took steps to soften the impact of declining revenue, tightening their control over budgets, reviewing the use of consultants, looking for ways to cut expenses, and considering cheaper alternative ways of doing their work. Francesca took none of these actions because she didn't see the context around her changing. She got a troubling performance review because she didn't adapt in response to the downturn—and she was sure she'd been treated unjustly for something that wasn't her fault.

Francesca didn't appreciate how her actions fit into the larger organizational system or how the organization fit into its changing market.

Women with low self-clarity are unable to adapt to business or performance realities because they don't see how they fit into the larger departmental or organizational context. Some are overly optimistic and so intent on overlooking the negative that they don't see they are headed for a major problem. One, for example, had such confidence in her abilities that she plunged happily into a job for which she was ill prepared. She kept saying that everything would work out in the end and that "if you think you can do it you will be able to do it." Positive thinking works much of the time—but not when you accept a job requiring advanced technical knowledge that you simply don't have. Unless you temper your optimism with a dose of reality, you can't respond appropriately to obstacles in your path. Many women took such pride in their strengths that they overlooked their weaknesses. When their shortcomings got them into performance problems, they were completely surprised.

Rejection of Feedback. Another problem often seen in those with lower self-clarity was unwillingness to seek or accept feedback. None mentioned any interest in getting feedback from coworkers. It wasn't that they were anxious about it. They just didn't value feedback. Of course, feedback from colleagues at work was a major ingredient in TWLP. Everyone got 360-degree feedback—but women low in self-clarity discounted it. Many were skeptical that others had anything worthwhile to say.

Some told us over and over again that their colleagues misunderstood them and were jealous; therefore, they didn't care that people saw them as needing to improve in certain areas. They knew more than anyone else about every facet of their work, so why listen to their critics? Others insisted that they couldn't trust anyone in their organization—every person who rated them was incompetent, so the feedback they received was useless. Both types were described by their coworkers as unapproachable in terms of feedback. They just wouldn't listen to others. And not only did they discount feedback from their coworkers, they also dismissed the feedback from the teaching staff and from the other women in the program. The staff couldn't possibly provide valid feedback because they did not work in the same industry, and the other participants were irrelevant because they were either too old or too young, or working in different functions.

Not only did those low in self-clarity dismiss formal feedback delivered in the program, they also stood out from the other women in that they never mentioned asking anyone for advice during the year when we interviewed them. They never saw themselves as owners of any problems. They blamed all their difficulties in life on others. One asked our interviewer why she should seek out advice or feedback when the problems were clearly her boss's responsibility. It is one thing to discount feedback from someone who is truly not capable, but if you feel no one in your office is qualified to give you feedback, then watch out. You may have an unrealized problem with self-clarity. There is almost always something to be learned from a work colleague telling you how your behavior affects them. Everyone has some useful feedback.

A common deterrent for low-self-clarity women was the notion that asking for feedback suggested that they might have a problem. These women have a point—asking for help or feedback does suggest you have an area of vulnerability. However, without asking for advice, suggestions, or feedback, it is hard to solve a problem or change your behavior. You spend too much time compensating for or correcting errors you could have avoided.

> Anna, as a senior vice president and the only woman at that level in her company, knew that she was looked to as a role model. She took that aspect of her job seriously. Anna feared that if she asked for help, others would see her as incompetent or ill prepared for her position. Anna told us that if you asked for help, you let others see that you were not perfect and she would never do this. She followed the maxim that to be successful, "you must radiate positiveness at all times."

So even those who saw some value in feedback struggled with the problem of getting it without showing vulnerability. This is a very real tension in organizations today when many women are still seen as pioneers for their gender in their line of work. If you ask for too much advice, you run the risk not only of labeling yourself as vulnerable but of so labeling women as a group as well. This issue is typical of minority members in all sorts of situations as they enter majority territory.

Others avoided feedback to protect themselves from being hurt. Often with good reason, these women were extremely guarded and did not trust colleagues to be compassionately honest with them— to give constructive feedback without trying to hurt them. As noted in Chapter Two, past trauma made a few of the women so protective that they let no one close enough to give them work-related feedback. This response was not universally the case; many had worked through the trauma and were as open to feedback from others as anyone else. But those who never addressed the severity of the trauma found it difficult to evaluate the source of the feedback and let their guard down, which restricted their ability to learn from their experiences and diminished their managerial potential over the long run.

Issues of Moderate and High Levels of Self-Clarity

Low self-clarity tends to produce dramatic problems like those discussed in the preceding section. Women with moderate and high levels of self-clarity tend to engage in subtler struggles, generally involving gender dynamics and the need to determine how personally to take tensions they encounter at work.

Understanding Gender Dynamics. As you rise in an organization, you run into its characteristic ways of dealing with differences between the genders. How does the organization view women? How high have women risen there? What are they rewarded for? Are there differences in how it rewards men and women? Are your own experiences related to these patterns? What opportunities are typically open to women? Do men get different opportunities? Are the opportunities you are getting typically given to women? Do the implicit views of leadership in the organization favor men and is this influencing your experiences? These are tough questions to ask and answer—but you must know the overall gender dynamics before you can tell if perceptions of you reflect the gendered environment or not.

> Hope was a high-performing, experienced nonprofit manager who worked in a highly political environment. When she was promoted during the year we knew her, she made sure she got the same authority, responsibilities, and privileges as the man who had preceded her—even though these were not initially part of her new job. She attributed the difference to gender stereotypes in her organization and quickly persuaded her new boss to put her on equal terms with her male predecessor. Further, she had a history of "invisible work" with relationships in the organization (see Fletcher, 1999), becoming the person to whom people went for coaching or to figure out how to resolve conflicts. As she was promoted, she requested that this work be made visible—that it be formally acknowledged both for her and for others playing similar informal roles. She insisted that her new job description and the associated evaluation criteria include her coaching work and behind-the-scenes conflict resolution.

Understanding gender dynamics is also important when it comes to understanding feedback. Many women are all too ready to blame any negative feedback on gender dynamics.

> Hannah used her company's gender dynamics to discount the feedback she received. She felt it was tainted because she had been rated only by men in a company that had never had a female vice president or president. When men described her as overly aggressive, she was ready to dismiss the idea—but women in the program also saw her as belligerent and hostile to people with different points of view. Hannah used this feedback wisely and took it as a sign that maybe she was too aggressive at work as well. After she went back to work, she started talking more with other women in her organization to figure out what was real and not so real about gender dynamics there.

In *Cultural Diversity in Organizations* (1994), Taylor Cox calls Hannah's difficulty "interpretive confusion." The term refers to having to ferret out which part of feedback is due to bias or prejudice and which part is real. As Hannah learned, consulting with other women about your behaviors is an effective way to reduce confusion about possibly gendered feedback. You need to sort out what part of others' reactions to you is based on your actual behaviors and what part may be the result of stereotypes of women in the organization.

Understanding gender dynamics is also very important when it comes to pushing back on the organization. To act as a change agent and push for norms more supportive of women, you need to understand how much of what you want to change is a function of systemic practices and how much of it is a reaction to you as a person.

Taking Professional Situations Too Personally. In today's fast-paced, highly charged world, it is very easy to overpersonalize tensions in business. It is a challenge to learn that coworkers are responding to your role as a manager and not to you as a person. It is also a challenge to realize that although you as a person may be kind, compassionate, and caring, you cannot always demonstrate these qualities at work. Learning how to see yourself in perspective can help you accept some of the harsher realities of your organizational role.

> Jess had to slash her unit's budget and resources. Jobs would be lost and favorite projects terminated. Although she made these cuts as fairly and inclusively as she could, her staff was understandably disappointed and shaken. Jess took their anger personally. Although she knew that objectively she wasn't at fault, she found it hard to separate her subordinates' reactions to the business situation from her understanding of herself. She struggled with learning how to see the situation in perspective. Jess felt she was a bad person rather than a manager facing a difficult economic scenario, and she took a long time to mellow out afterward.

It is very difficult to separate out the parts of the manager role that may require doing things that you know will seriously upset others from the sense that you are a good and caring person. The clearer you are about your own nature, the smoother the process will be.

What Does Self-Clarity Look Like?

You always know when you meet people high in self-clarity. It is apparent that they know themselves quite well and that they know how they fit into the larger world.

Sees Patterns in Life

First, the woman who sees herself clearly can describe patterns in her life with insight. She knows how she responds to different situations and is aware of mistakes she has made in the past. She uses this knowledge to keep herself from repeating the same mistakes over and over again. She reflects on her experiences and uses these reflections to increase her self-knowledge and guide her behavior as her situation changes.

Amy is an extremely dynamic and intelligent manager with a strong personality and presence. Her high level of self-clarity has facilitated her growth on all the themes. At the time we worked with her she was new in her job, but she'd long been a leader in other well-known organizations, recruited from one to the next because of her outstanding track record, brilliance, and personal warmth. Amy's desire for a career and graduate education had come as a surprise to her parents, who had raised her to be a good wife, mother, and housekeeper. She did marry and have children, but she kept her career on the front burner all the time. Amy had realized early on that she was a perfectionist trying to excel on all fronts, and she learned that this approach didn't work for her—she gained weight and suffered from a variety of stress-related diseases.

In response to these problems, she started paring back—she gave up ironing her husband's shirts, hired a housekeeper, bought take-out, and—most important—learned to delegate well at work. In addition to structuring her life in a way that supported her many goals, Amy also changed her thinking and consciously decided not to be so hard on herself. She learned to set more realistic expectations and, in doing so, removed a lot of anxiety from her life. With each promotion in a company or move to a new one, she learned more about how to fashion her life effectively. She was very aware of her workaholic and perfectionist tendencies and structured each new position she took on so that she wouldn't fall prey to her desire "to do it all."

Amy came across as extremely centered and was one of the few women in the study who, despite a relatively high organizational level, was able to take time for herself and maintain a strong family life. She found a lot of joy and peace in her life and did not feel guilty about missed opportunities with her family or at work. Despite her many career advances, she hasn't taken everything on offer. Instead, she's turned down some opportunities because she thought it would be impossible to maintain the wholeness of her life and handle the job at the same time. She is well aware of her tendency to be a workaholic and shares this knowledge with others, asking them to help her keep it in check. Amy focuses on the patterns she creates in her life and repeats those she has enjoyed in the past while avoiding those that have caused problems.

Oriented to Learning. Women high in self-clarity usually describe themselves as lifelong learners. They approach new situations as opportunities to learn and see difficulties as a challenge.

> Amy learns about herself from each transition and takes responsibility for her own learning. She admits when she makes a mistake and tries to grow from it. She says she tries to shape her actions from what she learns about life: "I'm working with myself to monitor how I'm feeling about what's going on with me, so I can maintain that growth. . . . I'm watching and waiting so that I know which of those opportunities fits who I am and where I want to go."

For Amy, self-clarity is a tool she uses to guide the direction of her life. She is extremely self-reflective and constantly connects her reflections to her actions.

Views Life as a Story. Women high in self-clarity generally see events as interconnected. They examine how the different pieces of their lives fit together and even see hardships as part of their own evolution. With this knowledge, they come across as fortified for dealing with new stresses.

> Amy tends to look at her life as a story playing out across time. Her decisions are made in the context of writing her life story, which provides her with a highly agentic approach to viewing her decisions. She evaluates each new opportunity in terms of what it would add to her experience base and carefully selects those that will build her capabilities without taxing her sense of wholeness.

Takes Advantage of Feedback. Women high in self-clarity use feedback effectively. They know how to take feedback from others and use it to refine, change, or confirm an understanding of themselves. They take feedback seriously, look to see how it plays out in their lives, and share it with others.

> Pam is a fifty-one-year-old manager who has learned to ask others for feedback on her behavior and how she is affecting others, and to use

that feedback to change her style. After the program, she shared her feedback with colleagues at work. She pulled out the reports and let people know what she had learned about herself. Pam also used her 360-degree feedback to confirm that she is well suited for and comfortable in her leadership role. The reinforcement she got from feedback encouraged her to take some risks she later reported were well received.

It is important to note here that feedback isn't Pam's only source of information on how she is doing in different situations. She is also very good at self-evaluation and can stand back from herself and determine how she is doing. Pam's internal compass is strong. She uses the feedback to complement her own self-evaluation. She does not substitute feedback for a strong self-assessment system; rather she uses it to enhance and check her own assessments.

Robin, a twenty-eight-year-old manager in the midst of a transition, used her feedback to refine her sense of what she was looking for. Although she was happy in her current setting, she was trying to decide if she wanted to stay in that company (which had recently reorganized) or move elsewhere. She used her self-knowledge to find an opportunity that suited her strengths and preferences and that would also push her to learn new skills—and she used both formal and informal feedback to refine her sense of self. At the time we knew her, she had several career possibilities. She investigated each thoroughly and thought about how she might fit into it. She took an approach of testing the waters by meeting with several people from the companies she was interested in and carefully exploring the dimensions of job offers. Over time she sharpened her focus on what she needed and used this to adjust her target and was able to negotiate offers that closely matched her goals. At the time of our last conversation, she had two good offers to consider.

Self-clarity helps women make choices consciously. Because they know themselves so well, they can make sound life decisions. It's not that everything is crystal clear all at once. For many the picture seemed fuzzy at first, but a woman with a strong sense of self knows how to bring the picture into focus. She knows her comfort zone and her likes and dislikes. She constantly evaluates the situation and options as well as what she wants and she will work to change situations and adapt her behavior if needed, until there is a good fit and she can perform effectively.

Understands Organization and Gender Dynamics. Self-clarity also helps women to understand the gender-related political undercurrents of their organizations.

> Anita, a fifty-year-old woman with two grown sons, tries to be very conscious of the gender dynamics in her organization. She understands how men react to her and realizes that she is sometimes seen as a mother figure—people much younger than herself sometimes expect her to solve their problems for them and to be extremely nurturing at all times. She guards against this and, while trying to be compassionate and understanding, steers others away from putting her in the mother and confidante role. She also promotes her own accomplishments so that her work gets the kind of light people don't typically shine on a mother figure. Like Hope, she campaigns to get credit for the work of coaching others. She says there are women's issues out there that affect the perceptions of leaders and it is important to acknowledge these issues.

Views Self Objectively. A further defining characteristic of a woman high in self-clarity is her ability to see herself objectively. She understands that she is separate from her work, family, career, and other duties. She has roles but she is not them. The woman high in self-clarity does not overpersonalize difficult business situations. She also does not lose herself in attending only to others, even though she has caring and connected relationships.

Moreover, she understands how her identity has been shaped by others—her family, her relatives and friends, her organization, her society. She knows her own value system and how it relates to the values of others. She knows when demonstrating her values may offend others. She lives with her own view of the truth and understands that friends, family, and colleagues may see the world differently.

> Kelly elected to give her ex-husband primary custody of their daughter in their recent divorce. She had always been the breadwinner; her ex had always been the homemaker and the main caregiver for their child. Kelly thought that yielding custody would be less traumatic for her daughter, who was used to her father's central role. As you might expect, many criticized Kelly for this and asked how she could do it. Kelly realized she was violating a cultural expectation and didn't get angry with those who questioned her decision. Accepting that values could come into conflict, she maintained strong relationships with those who disagreed with her— even with her beloved grandmother, who felt a mother should never live apart from her child. Kelly realized her grandmother was raised in a different time and place and had different values.

How Can You Develop Self-Clarity?

Developing self-clarity is an ongoing process. Even if it is one of your strengths, you need to keep seeking ways to further refine it. We found that the people working most actively on self-clarity were the ones who already had the highest levels. These were also the women who were regarded by their peers as most effective on the job. Conversely, it was the women who got the poorest performance ratings from their colleagues who ignored this area. They were doubly troubled; they had problems and could not see them.

So, how do you refine your sense of self-clarity? Exhibit 5.1 summarizes what the experience of the top-performing women suggests.

Seek Feedback

Feedback can be informal or formal. Ask for informal feedback from your friends, colleagues, and family with regard to a specific skill, situation, or decision point. Ask for feedback about how you are doing and what they think you might do differently. Listen to

---

EXHIBIT 5.1. A Developmental Thumbnail for Understanding and Achieving Self-Clarity.

1. Seek feedback.

2. Examine your behavior.

3. Look for patterns in your life.

4. Pay attention to your organizational environment.

   • Take note of changes in the climate.

   • Find out what happens to other women.

   • Ask others for their take on the environment.

5. Make self-learning a priority.

---

what they have to say. An important element of making feedback effective is that the recipient hear it clearly. You may want to reflect back what you heard to gain further clarification of what people are trying to tell you. Once you understand the feedback, then you need to actually use it to enhance your self-knowledge and shape your behaviors.

Celeste is wonderful with clients and great at selling the services of the large consulting company she works for. Recently, she began managing a group of consultants within her area of expertise. Things went well at first, but she started getting bogged down in administrative details. She assessed her own performance and became concerned that her haphazard scheduling and budgeting would be a problem. She asked for informal feedback from her staff, a former boss, and some customers, who all confirmed her self-evaluation. Everyone said she was great with customers and in selling the business; her former boss even called her "the rainmaker." However, projects were getting off schedule and her budgeting process was beginning to cause conflicts. Although this wasn't what Celeste hoped to hear, she agreed with the assessment and thanked her associates for their honesty. One of her friends recommended hiring an assistant manager to handle more of the administrative and systemic role while Celeste worked her magic with clients. Celeste tested this idea with a peer who was a friend and with her former boss. Then she tested it with her current boss, staff, and clients, who all thought it would work—and it did. Although she wasn't proud of her lack of interest in the administrative side, she accepted this as part of herself and worked to partner with someone who could deal with it. She had gained a sense of confidence and empowerment that stemmed from understanding her performance strengths and weaknesses.

Informal feedback is one option; formal feedback is another. Many companies use multirater feedback (also known as 360-degree feedback), which asks people with different vantage points (bosses, peers, and direct reports) to rate the subject on a set of managerial skills and abilities. The results are typically discussed with a professional coach or management-development expert. This structured feedback is a great way to enhance self-awareness. If your company doesn't offer it, you can seek it elsewhere. Many leadership or professional development providers offer it.

Examine Your Own Behavior

Not only did women high in self-clarity take outside feedback into account, they also excelled at evaluating themselves. They had well-developed performance standards to judge themselves by and they worked to make those standards realistic. If you want to develop self-clarity, pause frequently to ask yourself how you are doing according to your own standards. How are you doing in relation to your goals? Have your goals changed? Do you see obstacles in your path? Can you change so as to overcome these obstacles? Where are you doing well? Monitor your progress on your goals over time, so you can determine when you are in trouble and begin a process of self-correction.

Look for Patterns

Spotting the patterns in your life will help keep you from repeating mistakes or running into the same old obstacles. Once you recognize what is going on inside, you can address situations before you hit major problems.

Journaling can enhance the process of refining self-clarity. There is no right or wrong way to do a journal. Some women write down what they learn, some note questions about life, some try to describe different situations, some describe the day's highlights, some try to resolve problems. The main point is that you use the writing to reflect on yourself in context. If you are having problems figuring out how you come across to others, journaling may help you see yourself more objectively and can give you some insight as to how you come across to others. You can also use a journal to broaden your awareness by recording feedback that doesn't seem clear, so that you can think about it later and perhaps put it together with other feedback in the future. You might even imagine you are some person in your life with whom you are having problems and try to describe your behavior through their eyes; doing this can sometimes surprise you with new insights. A journal can be a wonderful place to play and experiment with new ways of looking at your life.

Pay Attention to Your Environment

As strange as it may sound, to see yourself clearly, you need to see where you are. Take note of changes in the organizational climate, including the small changes that seem unlikely to influence you—sometimes they show trends or add up over time. Note what happens to other women and to people in situations similar to yours. Try to understand the gender issues in your organization. How do people treat working mothers and pregnant women? How do they treat women who are very attractive? Is extra work given to young, childless women? Do older women get their chance to shine? What are the leadership norms? Do they implicitly favor men? What are the policies about family leave, maternity leave, and childcare and elder care responsibilities? Look for patterns and notice when those patterns might relate to gender, so you can be prepared for the ways some of your needs and preferences might be received by others.

Colleagues, friends, and family can aid you. Some of the work of self-clarity has to do with figuring out what you are contributing to a difficult situation and what the environment is contributing. If you are facing a challenge at work or in a relationship, ask others to help you see what you may be adding to the problem. If the problem seems to reflect systemic gender or political dynamics, then you need to work with others on understanding these dynamics. Network with people who are in similar situations so you can figure out the lay of the land. Use others to interpret the context. Ask peers about their experiences so you can see if your problem is part of a trend. After TWLP, many of the participants in the study met with colleagues to informally check out their sense of the organizational climate for women. Once they understood the climate and their own situation relative to systemic gender issues they were better able to deal with problems. The goal here is not to figure out where to place the blame, it is to find effective means of reaching important goals in your work and life.

Make Self-Learning a Priority

Do whatever you can to focus on continuous learning about yourself. If you make a mistake, view it as a learning opportunity. Ask what went wrong. Try to see how things could have turned out differently and how you might have acted differently to make that happen. Think about what you got from an opportunity, even if it didn't work out the way you would have liked. Focus on the job challenges you face. Can you view these as opportunities to learn something about yourself, your work, or your organization? Take advantage of activities that promote insight—self-help books, formal development programs, personality inventories, coaching. If you keep a journal, write down the things you learn and the story about how you learned them. What happened that taught you this? Your learning is a treasure that you build throughout life; the journal can be a way to keep that learning fresh and available to you over time.

Obstacles to Self-Clarity

Gaining self-clarity sounds easy enough on the surface. In actuality, it is quite difficult. As discussed earlier, one of the tough parts about developing in this area is that those who need it most are least aware of it. People grow used to a certain level of self-understanding and don't realize that it could be better. Unfortunately, a lack of self-understanding can block development across the board. The best advice we can offer is that if you think you wouldn't benefit from growth in this area, you are probably wrong. All the women with strong self-clarity continued to work hard at looking for patterns and at understanding their needs, drives, and abilities. Since some of these things change throughout life, it takes ongoing attention to keep in touch with what matters. Again, it was the women who needed to grow in this area who tended not to realize that they had development work to do.

Even if you want to develop more self-clarity, many obstacles can get in the way. Feedback is an important resource, but constructive, helpful feedback is sometimes hard to get. Many women had bosses who were incompetent at giving feedback, and some had bosses whose feedback was destructive, unprofessional, and abusive. These bosses seemed to have no idea that the purpose of feedback is to improve performance, not to punish or ridicule. It is hard to develop an accurate sense of self when you are slammed day after day.

> Lee needed feedback badly but what she got was badly delivered. Her boss seemed to have a prejudice against women; he never mentioned her strengths. Instead of giving feedback privately, he chewed her out in public. His feedback was mostly negative and delivered with anger and hostility; she had no chance to defend her actions. Obviously this was a lousy learning situation. It wasn't just the negativity that made

the feedback a problem; it was also that it was delivered so poorly. Lee was devastated and felt powerless to change the performance problem she was having. Despite all the feedback, she still didn't understand what she was doing that was ineffective.

What can someone in Lee's spot do? A few measures offer some hope.

One step Lee took was to enter the program in which we met her, where she could seek out 360-degree feedback and have it reported to her by professionals with expertise in management development. The feedback in the program helped her to discern what part of her boss's criticism was on target and what part was off-base. She did learn later that her colleagues shared some of his concerns about her work but they disagreed completely with most of his other complaints. She developed a plan to address the areas in need of bona fide growth.

Lee also sought others' perceptions of her situation. She asked her peers if they also experienced the boss this way. She checked with other women to see if they felt similarly treated. They helped her figure out what part of the manager's message had nothing to do with her. Lee did some checking on her boss and she learned he had had a sexual discrimination complaint brought against him earlier in his career. She felt better knowing she was not unique in her experience of him and was able to see the situation much more objectively.

Sometimes it is not simply the boss who puts obstacles in the way of developing self-clarity—the overall organizational climate can do the trick as well. Again, part of self-clarity is understanding yourself in context. If the context is hostile toward women and systematically undermines their growth, then it is harder to get a clear picture of yourself and others or to grow toward your own potential. Further, a hostile environment makes it much harder to handle interpretive confusion. The presence of prejudice means that a woman manager constantly has to figure out what role prejudice plays in others' reactions to her and the feedback she gets from them. Networking within the company is the best remedy for this—you need to rely on joining with others to figure out what is going on. This is what Lee did to check on her boss. It can also be useful to ask colleagues outside the organization to help you understand your situation.

In addition, organizations hostile to women tend to have few women in managerial positions, so the ones who are there may have no access to role models and no reference group with which to validate their perceptions. It is tough to be a lone woman in a complex, unfriendly situation.

> Ruth, who manages an engineering group, says she can't really relate to anyone at work because they are all men. She feels pressure to act like a man and to avoid acting too much like a woman. It has been hard for her to fit in. Not only is she the lone woman, she is one of the few without children, which makes another dimension on which she is different. Sometimes she feels she is going crazy. She has no one at work with whom to discuss issues of growth. She thinks the situation is further complicated because the men don't know how to work with her—they act prejudiced in part because they've never seen anyone treat a high-ranking woman without prejudice. Ruth feels that she can't be open at work and can't ask for feedback especially as the culture does not encourage open communication. Further, she says they would offer her only a funhouse mirror—one with lots of distortion, where she could not find herself.

What should you do if you work for a company like Ruth's? Again, one answer is to use other people to help you understand the situation. It might help Ruth to join a professional group for women engineers. She needs the validation of knowing that others experience the same sorts of things. If you are in such a trying environment, you need to share it with others with whom you share some similarities. You will feel better simply comparing notes and hearing about the experiences of others. Second, you could ask women in similar situations in other companies how they deal with the things that happen in their workplaces. Third, you can use a formal feedback program as Ruth did or engage in other activities to promote self-insight as discussed earlier.

The temptation to stay with the status quo poses another obstacle to the development of self-clarity. Exposure to changing circumstances enhances personal learning and development. It is difficult to learn more about yourself if your life is in a rut. New experiences, places, and people force you to confront yourself in new ways. But don't let lack of change keep you from learning more about yourself. Seek out situations that will make you reexamine yourself. Travel. Meet new people. Discuss things with people whose ideas differ from your own. Seek out people raised in other cultures or countries. Think about what you learn when you're experiencing a change.

A final obstacle to gaining self-clarity can be sheer distraction. If you are going through marital problems, elder-care problems, child-care problems, serious health problems, and so forth, you may well overlook or discount feedback. It is extremely difficult to focus on your own development during periods of crisis and trauma; we didn't observe anyone able to do this. Of course, overlooking self-development during turbulent periods may be totally appropriate— you may need to keep yourself as stable as possible when your life is in a major state of flux. On the other hand, if you remember that the quest for self-clarity is worthwhile, you can enhance your likelihood of returning to it when things settle down.

PART TWO

Next Steps for High-Achieving Women

There's a Hole in My Sidewalk: An Autobiography in Five Short Chapters

---

I
I walk down the street.
There is a deep hole in the sidewalk.
I fall in. I am lost . . . I am helpless. It's not my fault.
It takes forever to find a way out.

II
I walk down the same street.
There is a deep hole in the sidewalk.
I pretend I don't see it.
I fall in again.
I can't believe I am in this same place. But it isn't my
    fault.
It still takes a long time to get out.

III
I walk down the same street.
There is a deep hole in the sidewalk. I see it is there.
I still fall in . . . it's a habit . . . but my eyes are open.
I know where I am. It is my fault.
I get out immediately.

IV
I walk down the same street.
There is a deep hole in the sidewalk.
I walk around it.

V
I walk down another street.

—Portia Nelson

6

Growing Through Life Experience

The poem that opens this part of the book aptly describes learning over the life course. It is encouraging because it suggests we do eventually recognize and learn to deal with the "holes in the sidewalk"—to identify obstacles and navigate around them. This theme was borne out in our experiences with these high-achieving women. Although we followed the group for only a year, we saw patterns in how women of different age groups approached life. Life is a journey—and most of us do get better at dealing with the bumps as we get older. The women of fifty and older in this study were extremely impressive. If they are typical, age and experience do give managerial women a strong sense of wisdom about life, smart ways to make choices, greater resiliency, and inner peace.

The various developmental demands change their relative importance depending on your age group. Certain issues are more central at particular ages. Furthermore, within the context of each theme—authenticity, agency, connection, wholeness, and self-clarity—the issues vary with advancing age and the responses grow more sophisticated. In our study, each successive age group appeared to have greater wisdom about navigating life than the next younger one.

Of course, the observed differences between the groups are not necessarily a result of age. Our study was cross-sectional, so the differences could be a function of changing opportunities and social norms rather than the aging process itself. Regardless of the reason for the differences, it is beneficial for you to understand variations in development in terms of these groupings. You can use this information as a rough preview of what the future may bring.

Differences Across the Age Groups

To think about issues of age, we divided the women into five age groups: 29–33, 34–40, 41–45, 46–50, and 51–55. These distinctions are not random. We based them on the work of Daniel Levinson, a psychologist who looked at the development of adults over the life span. He built his theory first on the experience of men (*Seasons of a Man's Life*, 1978) and later verified it with women, as described in *Seasons of a Woman's Life* (1996). Levinson argued that adults go through a process of developing a life structure and then questioning and revising it, in alternating periods throughout the life span as they develop and grow.

Women's lives do vary—they don't share a lockstep progression. Childhood experiences, life events, and current family status all influence developmental themes. Despite the myriad ways life can play out, however, we found it was still useful to use the age markers to create a general sense of the development of managerial women over the course of their careers.

Women Aged 29–33: Married to My Job

This is a very busy and exciting time of life for managerial women. The nine young women in this age group had high-powered jobs and were making a difference in the corporate world at a relatively young age. All nine were college graduates, and six had master's degrees. They had titles like director, project manager, or project engineer. Their marital status varied, with some never married, some married, and some undergoing a separation. If married, they often had husbands who were in transition at work, with job changes, promotions, or transfers. During the year we knew them, they were a mobile group. Five of them changed residence during the year. Three received big promotions.

Agency was the dominant theme in the lives of these women. Virtually all were very intense in the pursuit of their careers. Women in this group are establishing the groundwork for an executive life, learning to take risks and have an impact on an organization. The majority of time in all three interviews was spent talking about their current major projects—their struggles, their accomplishments, and the visibility resulting from leading a high-profile initiative. They work extremely hard—long hours and weekends. They see their current assignment as a stepping-stone to an executive career. They scan the environment for future tasks, projects, and assignments that could help them achieve their goals. They have a life plan that revolves around their career. Women aged 29–33 seek out developmental opportunities to enhance their capabilities. If you are in this age group, it is likely that this is a highly agentic period of your life, with agency directed toward your career goals.

> All Jessica wants is to do a great job. She came up with her project (an engineering idea), sold it to top management, and got the necessary buy-in and resources. She sees this as a chance to grow professionally and is using it to make herself known to higher-level executives. She has gained a lot of confidence from this project.
>
> Through this work, Jessica—who was already quite agentic—is learning to be even more so. This project has pushed her to take risks, and she has grown very bold. Jessica has used the project as a platform for getting to know people and has strengthened her delegation skills by working with the team assigned to her. She feels she is proving herself here and promoting her career in the company. Delegation has allowed her to carve out time for networking and learning about the political side of the organization. When she talks about growth, it is in terms of developing professionally and exerting greater influence in the organization. With most of her energy and resources dedicated to work, Jessica, like most in her age group, is not concerned with issues involving wholeness or authenticity.

These women are working to show they can succeed in a career so that if they later decide to have children no one can say they are not career-oriented. Even those who already have children are working endless hours because they want to prove themselves relatively early in their career. Wholeness manifests itself in terms of concerns about spending too much time at work and not having enough time for themselves or family members and friends. However, they don't seem as distressed by the issue as some of the older women are because they don't focus on what they are missing. Even when they say they want to be more balanced, they tend to avoid making the changes that would let them work less and attend to other things. They have a lot of self-discipline and are willing to sacrifice life outside work to create the foundation for a high-level career. They seem to trust that there will be a time when they will get around to other things.

Authenticity also pales in comparison to agency. To some degree, choosing a field and career path has provided a basic sense of authenticity. These women are living out an important life goal—that of having a managerial job with room for career growth. Beyond that they don't try to align their lives with their needs. For most of them, the arrangement seems to be working. They have not yet recognized obstacles they can't overcome. Such women take little time for themselves and don't seem to mind much. They sometimes have goals regarding exercise or hobbies and may even start one of these activities, but they drop it relatively quickly. Focusing on needs beyond career building is difficult. They recognize that they have personal needs, but they subordinate these needs to that of excelling at work.

They feel little conflict between the organizational definition of success and their own. External measures—pay, status, responsibility level, number of direct reports—have great meaning to them. They recognize that other values also matter, but feel little need to redefine success based on their own standards. Their happiness is largely based on professional life, and though they know that this may be detrimental over the long term, they are not ready to channel energy to other aspects of life. These women give a lot less attention to authenticity than the older women do. They either don't see it as an issue or they derive authenticity from their careers. They are just starting to reflect on what is important to them besides work.

Connection also seems secondary to agency. At this age women value relationships but rarely pay much attention to cultivating them and achieving greater intimacy, and they do little to develop new ones. They express love for husbands and other family members, but also seem to take them for granted. "I pulled some hundred-hour weeks for that project," said one, adding, "I put my husband on hold." When they have difficulties, they do rely on family members for support and encouragement. Friendships are enjoyed but not emphasized as much as work.

Organizational relationships are purposeful. They are starting to learn to use others as role models by watching successful men and women at work and emulating their actions. Further, these women are also learning the value of developing good relationships with peers and are practicing lateral influence, reaching out beyond their function to create a network of support, and are also trying to create greater visibility upward in the organization to enhance their career prospects. They rarely join the older women in making strong goals with regard to personal connection. Work is so dominant in their lives that they have no time to strengthen connections for the sake of relationship values only.

Very few of these women recognize self-clarity as an issue. They usually know their strengths better than their weaknesses and some are confronting performance issues for the first time in their lives. Some seem to be in denial about performance issues, questioning feedback from others and wondering how they could be getting negative feedback. One said she had always been "the golden child" in her department; she could not understand why she was having performance difficulties now. She didn't seem to appreciate that as you move up the corporate ladder, the skills that once brought success may not help you cope with your new challenges. In terms of the poem, she has fallen into the hole in the sidewalk for the first time; it's not her fault and she can't see her way out. There is, however, a lot of variety among the women in this age group in their approach to self-clarity, and some are already adept at identifying and adjusting their own patterns of strengths and weaknesses.

In terms of understanding gender dynamics, they are more uniform. They are just beginning to realize its impact on their lives. Although they haven't hit the glass ceiling yet, they can see how it has trapped others. They look to older women as role models for successful navigation. They are also trying to figure out how to be a manager without acting either too masculine or too feminine. They fear that having a baby will make them appear less career-oriented, but they aren't sure how to handle this other than to work really hard to show their dedication.

Women this age also seem to be trying to learn not to over-personalize events at work. Since their career matters so much to them, they take every setback deeply. During the year we kept in touch with them, many spoke of learning to separate their identity as a manager from their identity as a person. But it is hard to deal with the disappointment when someone higher up in the organization rejects a piece of work you invested yourself in. The women in this group are figuring out how to deal with negative feedback constructively and to put it in perspective.

Women Aged 34–40: Branching Out

This was the largest age group, with twenty-three women. They had a variety of family structures: 29 percent were single and 71 percent were married or in a committed relationship; 46 percent had children. They are well educated, with a relatively high percentage (42 percent) having a master's degree. Women in this age group are often in transition, and many face the first significant encounter with a career obstacle. Over the course of the year, 30 percent changed residences, and 43 percent started looking for a new job. (The latter is the same percentage that reported organizational restructuring; the groups were not entirely the same, but there was a great deal of overlap.) Life has a lot of uncertainty for this group of women.

Agency still matters. They keep working on career goals and contemplate what it will take to reach them, seeking to move from junior positions to more senior ones. Some see that their career isn't blooming as they dreamed. Reorganizations may have removed a target position, disagreements with senior managers may have slowed progress, or they may simply have come close enough to the glass ceiling to feel its effects personally. In response, many add to their career goals by taking on a new role or a new job. However, in the process they adjust their lives so as to be both more authentic and realistic. They focus on how they fit with the job not just in terms of skills but also in terms of personality and lifestyle. They redefine and modify their strategies so they can expand their lives beyond work. Other themes take on more significance. Agency in career goals, though still important, no longer dominates the agenda.

Connection is more important to these women than to the younger ones. Life has expanded beyond career and their involvements focus on other people as well as on work. They tend to set goals that include friends and family, and they vow to spend more time with their loved ones and friends. Single women are intent on adding intimacy to their lives. One manager said, "I have become totally rootless, in other words, I have no roots anywhere." She had moved so many times for her career that she felt all alone, and her new goal was to be more settled. During the year she talked with us she changed jobs to gain a stronger connection with her family.

The focus on connection carries over at work as well. These women try to be more personable with their staffs and work on networking specifically with women in their own and other organizations. Some of them have reached levels with few female peers and they seek to develop supportive relationships with managers facing similar issues.

Authenticity also steps up in importance for this age group, who begin to think about ways to get their lives better aligned with their values. Life is complex enough to make them reassess even long-valued priorities. Several initiated job transfers to other companies or branches as a way to improve the alignment between their work and their needs and preferences. However, many were unclear about how to achieve the level of authenticity they desired.

Wholeness is the dominant developmental theme for this age cohort, and usually involves substantial pain. As their family life becomes more demanding, these women often describe themselves as "fragmented." They try to reevaluate their priorities so as to feel more whole. They've begun to see that having it all has a price tag, and they long to feel better integrated. But if they do cut back at work, they feel insecure. Meanwhile, single women question what else there is besides work. One said, "I have a great career but nothing else going on in my life." In terms of the poem that opened this part of the book, both groups see the hole but aren't doing anything to get out or go around. Although they are in turmoil, they are hesitant to change their behavior to address the issues.

Self-clarity still seems secondary. However, women in this age group are starting to talk about the different ways men and women are treated in their organizations. They start to consider this context in relation to their own experience. They also begin to see their lives in totality and develop long-term visions as to how they would like to grow. Self-descriptions demonstrate a relatively long-term perspective: "Maybe I can't have it all at the same time but I can have it all at different times."

Women Aged 41–45: Getting Comfortable in My Own Skin

Of this small cohort (seven women), 87.5 percent were married and 62.5 percent had children. There were a number of changes going on in their work lives, with 71 percent reporting improvements. With regard to personal activities, 86 percent noted that they started a recreational or healthful activity during the year we knew them; they took up such things as exercise, music, sports, and art.

Agency is still a developmental theme, but the focus is less on career and more on other life goals. These women restructure their lives to focus on what is most important. They exert control over their lives and start shaping their environments so they can have as great a sense of well-being as possible. Instead of leaving difficult situations, they are more inclined to fight back and set boundaries and conditions that are more satisfying. One said, "Even if I lost my job and income, it's okay. . . . I am being a proactive advocate for myself versus being a victim or reactor to circumstance. You know, that I have the power to kind of steer this shift within me." If they fall into the hole, they will know how to get out!

Authenticity is the dominant theme for this cohort, which is part of the reason their agency is active in multiple life domains. These women work actively to ensure that their lives and their values are aligned as closely as possible. They rarely sit back and accept the status quo. They make career decisions without seriously compromising personal goals. In contrast to the younger women, they place greater value on internal measures of success than on the organization's yardstick. When dual-career issues come up, these women can create solutions that help both spouses achieve their goals—sometimes with some friction, but they know how to work things through with their husbands. Women in this group also excel at using boundaries to ensure that they live life according to their priorities. They keep the promises they make to themselves.

Jill, for example, is looking for a new job after organizational restructuring left her facing a high-growth job offer with elements that violated her values. She said that earlier in her career she would have taken whatever was offered just to stay in the company. Now she will only take on a job that she feels both fits her values and provides opportunities for growth. If that means leaving the system, so be it. She has focused on what she wants for herself and is determined to get it. Life experience has given her confidence that she can survive.

Connectedness is also a priority. These women value relationships and work on strengthening them. They look for ways to make new friends, and they stay in touch with old friends, nieces and nephews, aunts and uncles, sisters and brothers. For example, one woman told us, "My brother travels a lot. We weren't always able to get together. We have kept in touch much more regularly than we were for a while . . . we have actually planned things where his wife and he, my husband and I would go out to dinner."

They want to become mentors, making it a goal to give back to the community of women some of the lessons they have learned. They find themselves attracting others to them and derive great pleasure from the mentoring experience. Furthermore, by coaching others these women reinforce their own strengths and their philosophy of life. They take responsibility for socializing other women to the organization.

In their own work, they are good at seeking out others to act as sounding boards and help them deal with difficult issues. They have peers they can share concerns and hopes with. They rely on others in a sophisticated way.

This is the first cohort with a relatively high level of self-clarity. The other groups were aware of their own strengths and weaknesses, but rarely saw themselves in the context of life experiences and the larger world. This group seemed to have learned what worked for them and what didn't. They saw things more clearly than the younger women did. They also valued personal growth and development. They were open to learning more about themselves through therapy, self-help books, and other methods. They had the confidence to review their lives and try to improve them. They clearly identified and surfaced gender differences in the ways their organizations treated people.

Lori was seeking to improve her influence with her male peers. She wondered if she was just too quiet and submissive or if her male peers were routinely dismissing her simply because she was female; they talked over her and cut her off. She struggled with being heard. Lori told us, "They don't know how to disagree with me, and maybe I don't know how to disagree with them. But they are short, they cut me off or they talk over me. I've had so much talking over lately, when I do kind of say 'Here is what I believe,' that there is just something, it feels like a male versus female thing. . . . I'm noticing that it is happening to other women too."

Wholeness begins to move to the front seat. One said, "This job is very important, but I'm not going to sacrifice everything else for it." She followed through on this and kept her job from crowding out other activities and roles. Primarily she strengthened her boundaries and actively said no to many tasks she thought would unnecessarily expand her time at work. Another told us how she'd refused to fly across country for a meeting that would cut into a planned vacation, offering to join via videoconference instead.

The women in this cohort have become better problem solvers. They can see different paths to a goal and pick the one that allows for the greatest feelings of wholeness. Those in the next younger group had the same desire for wholeness but were not so effective in taking action to limit the encroachment of work on personal time—perhaps because they didn't see alternatives, perhaps because they didn't feel they had enough organizational capital to suggest alternative approaches. Women in their early forties have realized that you can't have it all at the same time and also have developed the initiative to carry out alternative strategies.

Women Aged 46–50: Growing in Wisdom

The different ways life can play out for high-achieving women were most apparent for this group of fifteen women: 53 percent had children, and 53 percent were married—though the two groups weren't identical, as three of the women were single parents. Some were dealing with school and chauffeuring and others were grandmothers. Obviously, the ages at which they had children varied widely. They also had a variety of educational backgrounds, ranging from no college to graduate degrees. Given the wide variety of life structures in this age group, we saw no common patterns other than a tendency to initiate new recreational or healthful activities.

This age group shows a resurgence of emphasis on agency as they reassess their careers and try to figure out what comes next. Some are developing strategies for taking their business in new directions. These women have achieved a significant management level and seek to make their mark on their organizations. They also want to exercise influence in a way that is truly beneficial to others, and to act as a model of leadership. They are focused on fine-tuning their lives to build a structure that will allow them to have a major impact before they retire.

Others focus on agency in terms of career-related and personal obstacles—organizational downsizing, marital problems, difficult adult children, husbands with career troubles. They seek to address these issues in an agentic way by identifying problems and dealing with them.

Anne works for a large multinational known for both its opportunities for women and its tendency to reinvent itself periodically through reorganizations. Despite the overall quality of the environment, however, Anne's situation was not ideal. Her boss was extremely difficult to work with and had not earned her trust. She also saw herself as a creative person and felt she had given up part of this in an attempt to fit in where she was.

Anne told us she had fallen into this hole before. She recognized the situation. The first time she had felt very helpless; now she knew how to get out. Spotting yet another realignment in progress, she wrote a compelling business case for moving her group—which would get her away from a boss she distrusted and would also give her license to be a little more creative. Although the lobbying process took the better part of the year, Anne finally succeeded in persuading senior managers to move her group into a new organizational home. She was proud that she instigated the move and happy with the results: a new boss who is well respected, easy to work with, and more creative.

Anne also worked on her personal life. Her marriage had been troubled for some time, and she and her husband had grown apart. She finally decided it was time to address these issues. She and her husband began seeing a counselor, and she told us that they were both putting energy into addressing problems they had ignored earlier.

Agency and authenticity seem to interact for women in this cohort. They fine-tune their lives to make life on and off the job more authentic. They actively work to obtain and preserve authenticity by either leaving inauthentic situations or trying to change their situations so they can act authentically within them. Anne essentially did both at work—she got out of the problematic reporting relationship and moved her job to a better-fitting situation. Similarly, in her personal life she tried to repair her marriage so she could feel more authentic in the relationship. These women are not passive; they evaluate difficult situations and act. They realize the importance of acting agentically when life throws curveballs.

Connection goals matter to this cohort but seem less intense than for some of the younger groups. These women tend to take a very matter-of-fact approach to connection, as if the possibility of not valuing it highly doesn't exist. Several mentioned expanding their circle of intimate relationships. They have strong connections with a handful of people and they want to expand their personal networks by renewing old relationships or creating new ones as a source of personal strength. Those with elderly parents strive to spend more time with them. Most give themselves permission to call personal friends from work—something that often seems inappropriate to younger women—because the frequent reorganizations they've endured have taught them that friendships outlast jobs. It now seems essential to well-being to maintain these social ties.

This group also values self-clarity and focuses on learning more and growing. They are attuned to gender dynamics and struggle to understand how gender issues play out in their work environments. Some of them openly discussed their experiences of sexism and discrimination. They have seen people enter, advance, and leave executive careers and have noticed women facing greater obstacles than men do.

As far as wholeness goes, we saw no clear pattern. The group showed a range of feelings about wholeness, with some feeling extremely lopsided and others feeling balanced and whole. This may be because women in this age cohort had a variety of family structures and life histories. They also varied widely in terms of their organizational commitments, with some working seventy-five hours a week and others being able to keep it to forty.

Women Aged 51–55: Making My Mark

With only four women in this cohort it is difficult to describe them as a group. We noted few patterns in life events among them. Two were married and only one had dependents to care for. One commonality among them is that they seemed uniformly happy and satisfied with life.

At this age some of the chief concerns of connection are how to develop younger women and how to use a sense of connection to be supportive of others. These women see themselves as senior in their organizations and they feel responsible for nurturing the next generation of women managers. More generally, connections in their personal life are a great source of joy.

They are highly agentic at work, demonstrating strong productivity. They deal with significant issues, involving strategic initiatives rather than particular projects. They have learned a lot over the years and they put that wisdom to work. Retirement is approaching and the possibility of a changing relationship to work motivates them to seek a crowning success—to go out with a bang and leave the organization better off because of their contribution.

Authenticity is a major issue, with many talking of honoring themselves. They decide to start or resume hobbies and actually carry through on these goals. They are very clear on their priorities and structure their lives in accordance with them, with no waffling. They seem comfortable with their own definitions of success and no longer care about the differences between traditionally male external measures of success and their own yardsticks. As they approach retirement, they seek a deeper meaning in life apart from work. One said, "As I grow older and I reflect on what is really success, it seems to me that what's really success is to be able to raise a child that will contribute to society in a meaningful way and that should really be my goal. And yes, I can have professional success based on how much I get paid and how much recognition, but what I really contribute to a greater scheme of civilization or whatever you want to call it—is what values I leave with this child."

Self-clarity is the predominant theme for the women of this cohort. They see patterns in their lives, understand the context, and act as models for other women. Their self-perception seems to be freeing in many ways.

> Blanche told us that earlier in her career she feared screwing up and worried about all she had to know to be successful in her job. She has since had many career successes and some failures as well. Now she says she knows that she can rebound from failure and can lead successful initiatives. This understanding of her personal history gives her great comfort. She no longer fears the bad times so much because she knows she can deal with them. This personal knowledge has helped her to participate at work in a more joyous, relaxed way. She believes that understanding her life history has freed her up.
>
> Blanche knows what has worked for her in the past, what spells trouble for her, and what to do to deal with setbacks at work. Thus armed, she feels better equipped for navigating life. Furthermore, her deep self-understanding triggers a desire to stay on this path of self-knowledge. Blanche says the more she knows about herself, the more comfortable she is. She actively pursues self-development.

Blanche reflects the continuing quest for self-knowledge characteristic of this group. These women excel at separating who they are from what they do. They can look at their work objectively, understanding that the role of manager is part of life, but life is much more than being a manager.

> Wholeness was an issue earlier in Blanche's life, but not any more. Part of this is because her children are grown, but part is because she understands her priorities and so feels more unified. She has realized you don't have to have every experience all at once. Over your life course, you can experience different fulfilling situations. Blanche feels a lot less stressed now than she did years ago. She says she has learned to focus on top priorities and let the other stuff go. Blanche does have elder-care responsibilities that weigh heavily on her, but despite this stress, she doesn't feel divided or torn. She is saddened by her father's poor health but doesn't feel split by her loyalties to her father and her organization.

Blanche and the others convey a comforting sense of inner peace. They radiate groundedness and centeredness. It's not that they have addressed all their needs or solved all their problems. But they have learned how to lead rich and rewarding lives in spite of disappointments and obstacles—how to balance agency and connection, and how to live authentically, feel whole, and grow in their sense of self-clarity. They understand how to redesign their goals to thrive in a changing world.

Getting Hit on the Head with a Hammer: The Power of Life Events

Although age has an impact on development, it is only one of many factors. Life is full of events that exercise equally powerful forces. Significant events can be good (such as marriage and childbearing) or bad (health crises, financial problems, loss of a loved one) or have elements of both. Such events often acted as lenses, magnifying what was important and encouraging growth.

Adversity takes many forms; it can trigger development on many fronts. For example, health problems bring wholeness and authenticity to the fore. Soul-searching really steps up after a brush with injury or life-threatening illness.

After a heart attack, Mandy realized that she wanted more comfort and pleasure in her life as well as better balance between work and family. She had saved up a lot of money for retirement, but decided that she was young enough to take some money from the retirement pot and use it to enjoy today. She decided that home renovations would give her and her husband a joint project, allowing them to spend more time together while giving her the comfort and household pleasures she sought. With this decision, she worked on both wholeness and authenticity. She also realized that what she wanted from work was to be an entrepreneur, so she started taking steps to make that happen— the entrepreneurial life was more authentic for her than remaining an influential employee, and it would allow her to control her own time better and work within her newly realized physical limits.

Separation and divorce often triggered growth, but there was no pattern to the nature of the growth. For some women divorce promoted self-clarity. They confronted themselves in a new way and recognized their contribution to marital problems. For others, divorce spurred growth in authenticity. They realized what was important to them and worked to fashion a more authentic life. Some described a desire for authenticity as one of the factors contributing to their divorce. They felt thwarted in the marriage and saw divorce as a way of reclaiming their soul. For others, separation and divorce reflected their growth with regard to agency, representing the ability to take control and craft a new and more satisfying life. Divorce was also associated with connection—the wish for a new relationship, to once again have an intimate relationship with a significant other.

Harassment at work was another issue. The pain in such a situation made it difficult to do anything beyond protecting and rebuilding themselves. These women worked on strengthening their ability to deal with obstacles. Harassment helped develop agency in the sense that it motivated them to get out of a difficult situation. It forced women to try to gain control of their lives when someone outside their control made them miserable. It also influenced their feelings of belonging to a group, thereby affecting their growth in terms of connection. Women who felt harassed at work implicitly felt left out. With the harassment blocking their ability to bond with the work group, they were left wanting to feel part of a more supportive, connected community.

Loss of a loved one triggered growth in many domains. The common response was that life is too short to fritter away, you have to focus on what you want. This led some women to realize that other people are precious, causing them to value their connections more. They refashioned their lives to make more time for the people they loved. For other women the loss of a loved one sparked growth with regard to authenticity. Their take was that life is too short to live inauthentically. They seemed to value their own existence more as a result of the experience of loss.

Relocation also triggered growth. Several women encountered dilemmas of connection as they looked to get established in a new setting. They focused on developing friendships and entering a caring community. They wanted to find and join a group that shared activities. They also worked on disconnecting from the old setting and leaving people who meant a lot to them. Some chose relocation to strengthen connections with family and friends, often as a way of increasing their sense of wholeness.

Becoming a mother through childbirth or adoption also leads to development. New mothers—even those with other children—struggled with issues of wholeness. The added responsibilities made them feel fragmented. This distress encouraged them to readdress what was really important in life. It put their choices in focus and led to concerns with authenticity as they worked to figure out the relationship of their families to their managerial careers.

Family Stage and Structure

In addition to age and life events, family stage and structure also influence how the themes play out, especially wholeness and connection. Whatever their own age, women with young children face great demands, and wholeness manifests itself as a sense of being torn between absolute requirements. Wholeness was also an issue for women who were single and did not wish to be, who felt lopsided because they had a fabulous career but nothing else. Again, age mattered less than did desire to be part of a couple. Not all the single women felt this way, but those who were unhappy about it focused on trying to feel more whole.

Connection is also tied to family structure. Depending on how close they were to their family of origin, women faced different issues regarding connection. Many who lived far from siblings or parents spoke of wanting to be closer to their families, to bridge the geographic and emotional gaps. Desires for connection also played out in terms of raising and nurturing children. Women grew in ability to relate and develop people through their childrearing experience. Elder care elicited other issues of connection. Many women had to figure out how to nurture and nurse their parents. Even though they weren't providing the primary day-to-day care, they had to take responsibility for seeing that their elders had appropriate care. Marital status obviously influenced connection as well, with some single women setting goals around either finding a suitable partner or becoming more comfortable with the single life. Married women also wanted greater intimacy, sometimes with their husband and sometimes with female friends. Single women had many of the close friendships the married women wanted. Adult women enjoy having good connections with family, friends, and partners, and those with only some of these connections sought to fill out the picture.

Continual Development

A key point resulting from this look at life experience is that high-achieving women usually grow throughout their careers. This should not come as a surprise. However, there has been very little attention to the growth of managerial women over the life course. The descriptions of the age cohorts suggest that women grow and learn with regard to our five developmental themes, in patterns that mirror the poem about the sidewalk: from not seeing a hole to seeing it to taking responsibility for it to working around it. Although it is difficult to disentangle the effects of age and cohort, it appears that each time high-achieving women see an obstacle reappear, they see it sooner and more clearly and therefore are better prepared to deal with it. A major difference between the age groups is that younger women spoke of *problems* and older women spoke of the *actions they took to address the problems*. As we age, we get better at setting and achieving realistic goals.

Although the developmental themes can all be important throughout life, we did note some connections between the different age groups and the degree to which a particular theme motivated development. Here are the dominant themes for each age group:

Life Stage	Dominant Developmental Themes
29–33	Agency: How do I get ahead in my career?
34–40	Wholeness: How do I keep my career from pushing out the rest of my life?
	Connection: How do I develop and maintain important relationships?
41–45	Authenticity: How do I redefine my work so it is more fulfilling?
46–50	Agency and Authenticity: How do I realign my life so it is fulfilling both personally and occupationally?
51–55	Self-Clarity: How do I continue to learn and grow?

Will your life resemble the patterns described here? When we first started this chapter, we joked about calling it "What to Expect: The Career Years." But adult life doesn't lend itself to the same predictability that child development does. Women's managerial development is influenced by the variety of life structures open to women, the variation in times to enter and exit the workforce, and the impact of social change.

Society is a major influence. As noted earlier, though we believe the differences between the youngest and oldest cohorts in the study mainly reflect the accumulation of life experience, it is also possible that some are due to changes in social climate. For example, when the oldest group grew up, the standard view was that fathers were breadwinners and mothers were homemakers. Women made the home a place of peace and order for their husbands, handled the housekeeping, and cared for the children. The younger women had different experiences—their mothers often worked outside the home and they knew of successful career women. Second, higher education was a standard expectation for the youngest women and their friends. The oldest grew up in a climate where it was a less uniform expectation that girls would go to college—and those who did go to college often joked of working for an M-R-S instead of a B.A. Medical advances in fertility control may create different experiences for women as well. Today, women in their twenties and early thirties have much better chances of delaying childbearing successfully than were available to those now in their fifties. This manipulation of the biological clock makes it hard to say if the youngest group will face the same issues as the oldest one at the same points in life. Add to this the changes in the economy, globalization, technology, government, the impact of September 11, 2001, and views of marriage, and very different life possibilities appear.

How will your life map out? Who can say? Life pathways are influenced by many factors—your own desires, family influence, unexpected events, and changing times. With so much variation, it is hard to identify what is constant. However, some trends do emerge. Different studies provide evidence that women develop greater well-being over their life spans, and support our findings that women grow more authentic and more whole and see themselves more clearly as they age (Helson, 1997; Helson & Moane,

1987; Levinson, 1996). The sense of well-being characteristic of Blanche and her cohort seems to be typical for more mature women from other populations and periods of time.

It is more difficult to talk about agency and connection. Both were strong for all the women, though they manifested themselves differently in the various cohorts. Most prior research has looked at women outside the managerial world, where agency has traditionally been associated with men and connection with women. The conventional wisdom, based on Jung's (1933/1950) model of personality, is that during the years of parenting, agency increases for men and connection for women. When childrearing is finished, there is a crossover and women develop in terms of agency and men in terms of connection. Managerial women, however, don't necessarily follow these theoretical templates. We saw both agency and connection increase in personal and career realms over time. It is hard to draw conclusions as to how similar these patterns are to those of other women since the women in our study were few in number and unusual in their commitment to long-term managerial careers.

Understanding Your Own Life Experience

Perhaps the most important message of this chapter is that managerial lives play out in myriad ways. This book identifies common paths of development, yet the lives of managerial women unfold with tremendous diversity as a result of accidents of birth and social origin, age, life events, and family structure. What matters to you is your own life and how it is playing out in terms of the five themes. Understanding helps you to identify and absorb your own life's lessons and to act upon your knowledge to improve your life and those of others.

We have a few recommendations here, sketched in Exhibit 6.1.

Look for Patterns

It is important to look for patterns in your life so you understand your own growth. This will let you spot the holes that keep appearing in your sidewalk. Once you know what you tend to do and

---

EXHIBIT 6.1. A Developmental Thumbnail for Understanding Your Own Life Experiences.

1. Look for patterns in your life.

2. Write a narrative—and envision a future.

---

what situations are hardest for you, you can take preventive action before you run into major problems. Drawing a lifeline like the sample shown in Figure 6.1 helps to do this.

A lifeline traces events, choices, and transitions, allowing you to look for long-term patterns. To create one for yourself, start by drawing a long line vertically on a blank piece of paper. Then think of key events to include: a significant choice you made, something that happened to you, or any type of transition in your life—college, jobs, significant projects at work, marriage, divorce, birth of a child, rejection of a significant opportunity, relocation, illness, the loss of a loved one, a business problem, a promotion, or any other major happening. Start putting these events on the lifeline and indicate the age you were when they happened. The time intervals don't have to be equally spaced. Put in what is important to you. Your lifeline won't look like anyone else's.

Now write in when you've hit major obstacles. They may already be on the lifeline in terms of events, but add them if necessary. Think back to the poem—can you find your hole in the sidewalk? Is there a problem you keep running into? Make note of it. Put each instance on the lifeline. What techniques have you used to deal with it? Have they worked? What else can you try?

Next, review the five themes discussed in this book—authenticity, agency, connection, wholeness, and self-clarity. Think about times when you felt particularly high or low with regard to each of these. Write these on the lifeline. They will probably coincide with much of what is already there. Remember to list the event that produced these feelings if it isn't already on the lifeline. Don't expect to have a high and low for each theme. You should, however, have highs and lows for at least two of the themes on your line.

FIGURE 6.1. Sample Lifeline.

Events	Age	The Themes	
Started college	18		
Met future husband	20		• High connection
Graduated from college and started first job	22	• Low self-clarity	• High agency
First promotion	23	• Low authenticity	
Got married and started business school	25		• High connection
Graduated from business school and started new job	27		• High agency
Promotion	29		• High agency
Birth of son	32	• Low wholeness	• High connection
Marital problems	33	• Low authenticity	
New job	34		
Divorce	35	• Low connection	• High authenticity
Relocation and promotion	36	• Low connection	• High agency
Second marriage	37		• High authenticity
Birth of second son	40	• Low wholeness	• High connection
Death of father-in-law	42		
Promotion	43	• Low wholeness	• High agency
Diagnosis of significant illness for mother	45		• High self-clarity
Promotion	46		• High authenticity • High agency

You need not limit yourself to a single high or a single low for a given theme. Over a lifetime, people have many periods that seem particularly high in authenticity, agency, connection, wholeness, or self-clarity—and many periods that seem low.

Once you get the lifeline completed, think about what it says about you. Are there trends or patterns? Does one theme seem to be motivating many of your decisions? Do the themes ever come into conflict? Share your lifeline with a friend or colleague and what it says about you.

When we do this in workshops, many managerial women notice that agency is their dominant theme. Their agency often comes into conflict with either authenticity or wholeness. For example, one woman who left a high-paying corporate job to move to the nonprofit sector described it in terms of a trade-off between agency and authenticity. Although she had great impact in the industry, she felt inauthentic in her corporate job. Another realized that her bad first marriage was driven by the desire for connection but her choice of a husband made her feel inauthentic. She was happy to report that her second marriage was high in both connection and authenticity. Women in their mid-thirties often report conflict between agency and wholeness. They want the inner peace of wholeness but feel they must trade off for the sensation of power and control associated with agency.

Look at the lifeline in Figure 6.1. This woman is highly motivated by agency. However, at several points in her life she had a conflict between agency and feelings of connection and wholeness. The birth of her first son made her feel high on connection and low on wholeness. She felt low on authenticity when her marital problems surfaced but regained authenticity upon her divorce. She has maintained high levels of agency throughout her career and is now trying to achieve high levels of wholeness as well.

Develop a Narrative

Writing out your life story is another way to appreciate your own development over the life course. Mapping out your story is a useful way of understanding the evolution of your life. One way to start is to create chapter headings referring to different life stages: 0–10 years, 11–17 years, 18–22 years, 23–28 years, 29–33 years, 34–40 years, 41–45 years, 46–50 years, 51–55 years, and beyond. In reviewing your life, ask the following questions: What were the most important parts of my life during this time? What significant choices did I make and why? What were my significant relationships? How did I spend my time and energy? Use these questions to guide the narrative for each chapter.

After writing the narrative you may find it helpful to reflect on the story and ask yourself again if you see any patterns. Do certain issues repeat themselves? What are your dominant developmental themes? It is also important to focus on what is left out. What else in your life would you like to include? Are there relationships you'd like to add? Are there experiences you'd like to have? Have you had feelings of lacking something or of longing for something at various times? Contemplating these questions helps you to figure out the next chapter of your life. Set goals on the basis of what you have learned about yourself. Go ahead and start writing your future!

7

What Can Organizations Do?

People all like to think of themselves as in control of their lives and able to control what happens to them. With this mindset, women tended to define issues they faced as their personal responsibility. Furthermore, in designing the study we framed the issues and questions as matters of individual choice. Our goal at the outset was to look at how high-achieving women respond to the choices and trade-offs in their lives, but it soon became apparent that the women's struggles were not purely private; they had their roots in a changing culture fraught with contradictions for their role as women. High-achieving women face difficult choices and trade-offs because they receive competing messages. "You need to work all the time to succeed here" runs up against "Don't sacrifice your family for your career." The cultural transition in women's roles means that people aren't sure what women (and men) need to do in the new configuration.

Organizations can do a great deal to help women develop into authentic, whole, agentic, connected, and self-understanding human beings—and organizations that do so should profit in terms of the increased effectiveness of their whole workforce, not just the women they employ. Although organizational structures and policies alone can't do the whole job—it also needs educational, governmental, community, and media initiatives—organizations can do much more than most of them presently do to effectively include women into the world of working professionals.

Definition of the Problem

From an organizational perspective, the basic issue is that high-achieving women must compromise to survive in careers patterned after the stereotypical male experience. Women in management are still expected to dress, think, and act like the men currently in leadership positions and to meet male norms of effectiveness—with no recognition of the different but equivalent contributions they may make. Thus women feel pressure to sacrifice authenticity and wholeness for success. Connections with others become compromised and weakened. Attempts at agency evoke discrimination and harassment. Attempts at self-clarity are distorted by the proliferation of stereotypes and prejudices.

This social context is a source of ongoing stress for women managers at all levels. Some strategies—discussed throughout this book—do help women survive in inhospitable working environments, but these additional survival tasks distract them and consume energy that they would otherwise put into their work. Organizations that want to benefit from the full resources of their female members will need to do their part.

How can organizations change to capitalize on the influx of women? They can remodel their cultures to incorporate the basic developmental values of authenticity, connection, agency, wholeness, and self-clarity. There is only so much that individuals can do to adapt—organizations need new approaches to developing and retaining talent. We suggest that these new approaches can benefit men as well as women, given the societal changes of recent years.

In the fifth century B.C. Protagoras claimed, "Man is the measure of all things." And little has changed in organizational life since then. Rapoport, Bailyn, Fletcher, and Pruitt (2002) argue persuasively that organizations rely on male standards and experience from earlier decades. These masculine norms—first discussed by William Foote Whyte in *The Organization Man* in 1956—inhibit the experience and contributions of women and contribute to cultures that emphasize the following:

- *Work is primary:* The "ideal worker" is totally committed to the organization. Personal and family needs never interfere with service to the organization.

- *Competition is good:* Organizations foster a win-lose mind-set rather than a cooperative one, and value aggressive self-promotion and personal ambition.

- *Individual achievement is all that matters:* The best employees make individual contributions; they are stars who don't need help from other people to be effective.

- *Rationality is supreme:* Decisions are to be made logically and only on the basis of fact, and displays of emotion have no place in the business world.

- *Dominance is natural:* Autocratic decision-making styles are preferred. Leadership exists only at the top of the organization and cannot be exerted from the bottom up.

Few men fully endorse all these norms—the norms themselves are outdated and it's a rare man who can put work first all the time. Nonetheless, they still underpin the ideology of much of corporate America's work systems, reward systems, and approaches to career development. Whyte did not focus on the maleness of these norms—it was taken for granted in the 1950s workplace that managers were male—but Rapoport and her colleagues are right. In applying these norms, organizations inadvertently favor an idealized masculinity and disadvantage anyone, male or female, with more modern values. Although American society no longer assumes that all men should work and all women should stay home, few organizations have redesigned their managerial development policies and structures accordingly.

It is time for female norms in general, and the developmental issues we have identified in particular, to be incorporated into the everyday environment of the managerial world. We are not suggesting that male norms be replaced, but rather that a wider variety of values and behaviors be accepted in how managers design their lives. We want to see the standards and norms of organizations refined and reshaped so that they allow for the development of authenticity, wholeness, connection, agency, and self-clarity. And there is growing evidence that men also want such changes (Grover, 1999). Even when supportive policies exist, few men are comfortable taking time off to attend events at their children's schools or to care for an elderly parent. Taking these issues into account will broaden and develop organizational cultures and contribute to everyone's effectiveness. Thus a central question for organizations is how to reshape the culture to move women from a situation of survival to one in which they actually thrive. We suspect that organizations that answer this question successfully are the ones likely to retain the most talented men as well.

Why It Matters to Organizations

A first step in talking about reshaping organizational culture is to explain why the development of women matters to organizations. An organization that removes or alleviates systemic barriers can enhance the commitment of women managers. The supportive climate that results can enhance the performance of the organization as a whole.

Organizational Climate and Individual Commitment

Organizations should and do care about the commitment of their workforce, and most organizations invest heavily in their human capital. According to the Society for Human Resource Management (2001), lack of attention to diversity issues can diminish an organization's return on its human capital if productivity and commitment decline because employees feel disregarded or time is squandered in misunderstandings and conflicts, and the organization may even have to devote significant financial resources to legal defenses and settlements relating to discrimination and harassment. Conversely, research has consistently shown that creating and maintaining a culture where all employees feel included and valued results in decreased absenteeism, turnover, and expenses for dealing with grievances, as well as increased motivation and commitment (Society for Human Resource Management, 2001).

Improved Gender Equity and Enhanced Organizational Performance

Another sign that organizational climate is important comes from the work of Rapoport and her colleagues (2002). Using an action research approach in which they partnered with the organizations under study, they identified assumptions that hinder both organizational effectiveness and gender equity. They offer a way to help organizations achieve the dual goals of gender equity and effectiveness by using dialog between employees to reveal and understand underlying assumptions, and they provide an experimental approach to finding remedies for identified problems. Gender equity refers to the extent to which an organization values both masculine and feminine norms. They learned that addressing the climate in terms of gender equity resulted in enhanced organizational performance.

Creating a Developmental Culture for Women

Creating an organizational environment that supports the growth and development of women managers is a complex task. People often think of organizational culture in terms of the human resource policies that establish specific practices. Indeed, such practices can be an important route for changing organizational culture, but they are not the only means. They need to be complemented by actions both at the level of top management and at the work-group level.

The importance of consistent support for the change process cannot be overemphasized. Joseph Potts (1998) queried over 7,500 employees about diversity practices in nearly two dozen organizations. He found that diversity initiatives uniformly deteriorated or failed if top management withdrew its support. Only top management can allow for the experimentation necessary for a real shift in the environment. Similarly, at the work-group level, supervisory and team member behavior must reflect and reinforce the policy changes.

We offer an approach to organizational culture that involves several interrelated levels of change, addressing each of the five themes in terms of the types of cultural features necessary to promote its development. These actions are mutually reinforcing. Just as the themes are intertwined, so are the courses of action to support them.

Authenticity

Authenticity has to do with being able to channel your actions so your life embodies your goals and beliefs. One of the key complaints of managerial women is that they often feel that their organization won't let them act on their authentic values. In fact, many women opt out of corporate America and start their own businesses to achieve greater authenticity, as Dorothy Moore and E. Holly Buttner report in *Women Entrepreneurs* (1997). Large organizations with embedded masculine values can leave women without reinforcement for their values and skills.

What can an organization do if it wants to retain women whose authenticity is challenged by the current environment? How does it support authenticity in its women managers?

Organizations would do well to develop cultures that jointly optimize personal development and organizational effectiveness—what Joan Kofodimos (1993) calls "a climate for self-realization"—so individuals can develop in ways consistent with their true talents and goals. People don't all have the same needs and goals or want the same things, and a climate of self-realization allows everyone to have different values and still maximize their contribution.

Several human resource practices aid self-realization. One is to offer multiple career ladders. Many organizations have one career ladder—you move up in management or not at all. Multiple career ladders let people advance without taking on more managerial responsibility, which is a blessing for talented specialists such as scientists and engineers. Systems for lateral transfer legitimize and reward a variety of career paths.

PricewaterhouseCoopers provides one example of a career progression system that considers both individual competency and contribution to the organization. Employees are encouraged and expected to develop the skills and abilities to handle more challenging roles. They may choose to build expertise in a single area or function or in multiple areas (Engoron, 1997). By having alternative career ladders, the organization broadens definitions of success. It allows managers to keep learning and growing in their work even though they may not be rising on the executive track. One participant told us, "To feel successful, I need to feel like I'm always moving. I don't mean moving up. . . . To me being successful doesn't necessarily mean being vice president. I could stay at this level as long as I kept having the opportunity to learn other things."

A second practice that fosters authenticity is the sabbatical, which allows employees to engage in an activity of personal value without leaving the organization permanently. In our study, a number of women had things they wanted to do outside work, such as write a book or join an advocacy program. Sabbaticals help managers fulfill these dreams, and they often return to their jobs refreshed, satisfied, and reenergized.

A third practice links personal goals with development planning. Most organizations have annual performance and development-planning processes, but few take the manager's personal goals into account. A system that did so would look for ways pursuing organizational goals can help the individual fulfill personal goals, and for ways pursuing personal goals can help with organizational goals. Doug Lennick, executive vice president at American Express Financial Advisors, uses a system of this kind (1999). He helps his staff identify what they want so they can act on those values on the job.

Lennick also demonstrates the type of role that a top manager can play in supporting and championing a human resource practice. He discusses his own experiences in linking his personal goals with development planning. He acts as a role model in this regard and encourages others. In fact, he travels to other organizations to share the work his organization has done to help individuals create alignment between their values, goals, and actions.

At the work-group level, supporting authenticity means honoring individuality. Supervisors and team members must realize that a given end result can be reached in many ways—and through a variety of leadership styles. Many women reported feeling they had to use a macho, command-and-control style of leadership to be accepted by their peers and boss and to be perceived as being in charge. Although narrow concepts of leadership are difficult to change, the effort pays off. Subtle pressures to perform one way instead of another often reflect ingrained style, unrelated to productivity or ethical conduct. At the same time, it is important to recognize that women vary as widely as men in leadership behavior. Organizations can help address the issue at this level by offering intercultural awareness and self-awareness programs to help employees understand the many ways of being effective and to teach them to honor individuals with effective styles that differ from their own. Organizations should also take a long, hard look at the criteria invoked in performance reviews to make sure they focus on performance rather than on style.

Wholeness

Building a whole and full life is a critical task that involves integrating personal and professional roles as well as attending to both agency and connection. Lack of wholeness poses two sets of problems for executive women: some become workaholics while others try to do everything. We believe that employees who avoid these extremes and manage to feel whole and comfortable will work better, stay longer in their jobs, and have better morale. As noted in Chapter Four, women with a commitment to multiple roles actually tend to have both higher performance and greater psychological well-being than do women with a single dominant role.

Our study is one of the first to provide concrete evidence that engagement in roles outside work may provide substantial benefits to the organization as well as to the individual. Our data suggest that individual wholeness is just one aspect of a mutually beneficial relationship between employees and their organizations. Engaging in multiple roles can also contribute to individual work performance and development as a leader, and that contributes to organizational effectiveness as well. There seem to be significant performance benefits to organizations that not only encourage wholeness among their employees but also provide support and encouragement for employees to integrate their personal and professional lives fully.

The variety of work-life programs currently offered shows that organizations do recognize that employees have lives outside of work. Typical programs and policies range from flexible work arrangements to concierge services and employee assistance and wellness programs. Some of the latter incorporate practices the women in this study reported had made them feel more whole, including meditation, fitness, and massage.

The Adolph Coors Company, for example, operates a wellness center that offers services such as massage therapy, acupuncture, stress tests, and classes in stress management and mind-body medicine. The company estimates it reaps a return on its investment of $1.24 to $8.33 for every dollar it has invested in the wellness program (Dutton, 1998). Chubb Insurance recognizes the importance of the relationship of its employees' personal lives to their careers, and offers a variety of alternative work arrangements such as flextime, shorter work weeks, job sharing and telecommuting, as well as other employee support mechanisms such as a paid time-off bank and snowy-day child care. These measures have helped improve employee retention and productivity (Graham, 1996). DiversityInc.com (Staff, 2001) reports that Prudential Insurance saved $8 million through increased productivity and retention and decreased absenteeism after it implemented its diversity initiatives, which include flexible scheduling, career development programs for women, and child-care and elder-care referral programs. They also report that Ernst & Young estimates that it costs 150 percent of a talented employee's annual salary to replace her if she leaves. Its Flexible Work Arrangements Program is estimated to have saved the company $9 million its first year by improving the retention of valued employees.

To be competitive in today's world, large organizations must offer these types of policies. However, distrust poses a major threat to their success. A 1997 study by the Families and Work Institute found that among employees of U.S. private-sector companies with a hundred or more employees, 40 percent are concerned that taking advantage of flexible work policies will be seen as showing they lack commitment and thus harm their chances for career advancement. Despite promises to support engagement in outside roles, employees know (or believe) that companies with such policies are only paying lip service to the new ideas. For policies that support wholeness to be used and to contribute to a changing culture, top management must demonstrate full support for the initiatives. CEOs and senior managers need to encourage women and men to take time for personal and family roles.

To override the impression that taking advantage of work-life policies hurts careers, senior managers must use them. Doug Lennick supports the American Express Financial Advisors' flextime program by playing basketball during the workday. He shares this activity with his staff and puts it on his calendar. At our own organization, the Center for Creative Leadership, senior managers take advantage of the flextime policy to attend to personal goals and family needs—and they talk openly about doing so. They bring in children when their child-care arrangements fall through. Executive participation legitimizes the use of flexible arrangements for the rest of the workforce; lack of it makes such programs almost useless.

Support for policies fostering the development of wholeness is needed at all levels, but it's particularly critical for supervisors and work-group leaders. This level offers the greatest potential for cultural change. Like top managers, leaders of work groups need to use the policies and make sure people know about it. One woman told us of a manager who took a planned vacation despite pressure to reschedule it—much to the satisfaction of many of his employees, who saw him as a role model. Most important, those in leadership roles should never penalize people who take advantage of work-life balance programs and practices—and those who try to discourage such participation, however subtly, should be held accountable for acting contrary to the desired culture change.

The supervisor or work-group leader could also work to understand what is important to each employee. When managers manage people rather than tasks, their conversations can shed light on individual needs for pay, promotion, and flexibility. Workshops can help managers learn how to motivate and coach diverse subordinates. Accountability is also critical. Employees' usage of whole-life programs can serve as a benchmark of the work group's progress with the initiative. At the same time, attending to personal development does not diminish accountability for organizational goals—it creates a more realistic plan to achieve those goals. Furthermore, supervisors and human resource professionals can hold developmental conversations with employees that incorporate discussions of learning outside the work environment and how that may translate into more effective leadership behavior on the job.

Organizations can create a safe environment at the work-group level, making it a place where employees can discuss challenges in balancing life's different domains. This may mean keeping an open mind and being willing to think creatively about how to get work done, which requires combining the goal for a more balanced life with the goal of greater effectiveness at work. In *Finding Time* (1997), Leslie Perlow describes how one company used work-life conflicts at the group level to identify and fix a major problem with organizational efficiency. The company's practice of spreading meetings throughout the day made it difficult for its engineers to concentrate on their own work. It also made it difficult for them to leave on a timely basis and attend to their personal lives. When the meetings were shifted to a designated time of day, the engineers completed more of their projects on time while enjoying better work-life balance.

The approach these engineers used is described by Rapoport and her colleagues in *Beyond Work-Family Balance* (2002) as an example of linking a gender equity intervention to organizational performance. This example focuses on the norm of wholeness— allowing individuals to have priorities outside the sphere of paid work. The company helped its employees combine personal agendas with organizational agendas, building both wholeness and effectiveness. Once the fundamental assumptions were recognized, it was possible to address the dual agenda of gender equity and performance.

Connection

Connection—the longing to be attached to others, to belong with others—is a fundamental human drive common to both men and women. Since stereotypes as well as the general literature on women stress the high value women place on connection, we expected the women in the study to feel well connected and to have amply strong relationships. For many, however, this was not the case. Some seemed uninterested in connection; others were interested but felt blocked in attempts to attain it. Some of the women struggled with feeling isolated on the job. Others struggled more generally with a lack of intimate relationships that they felt was created in part by their extreme emphasis on career and the extraordinary demands of high-level corporate life. These situations can be addressed by modifying the organizational culture to better support the desire to develop connections with others.

Formal mentoring programs can help organizations support connection (as well as learning and development) among isolated managers. In addition to information and advice, a good mentor can provide support, encouragement, and protection and can facilitate connections with others. Sometimes a strong bond forms between mentor and protégée; they get to know each other well and become invested in each other's careers. A program that encourages cross-divisional, cross-functional, or cross-gender mentoring can help break down barriers between groups and increase feelings of connectedness.

Organizations can also strengthen women's feelings of connection by creating, developing, and recognizing both formal and informal networks. Many organizations support internal employee resource groups defined by ethnicity or gender. Other networks may cross organizational boundaries and provide connection through professional or technical support groups in various industries and companies. For example, we heard several women speak of benefits they derived from the Society for Women Engineers. As well as allowing them to help other women and be helped by them, participation in the group gave them more opportunities to speak in front of groups, interface with upper management, and gain visibility. The society developed a mentoring program and its members worked with senior executives and human resource managers in their organizations to garner informal company support for the program. Another company created an informal group of women to advise the mostly male executive team on issues and policies relating to women. In addition to providing visibility and networking opportunities for the women, this technique offered a way to bring senior executives and company policies up to date on women's needs and perspectives.

We urge organizations to take the next step and move beyond formal mentoring programs and networks to develop a culture that encourages mentoring and networking in general and also rewards people who do connective work. To this end, organizations can congratulate and reward *teams* for their accomplishments, not just team leaders. Team-based rewards—group bonuses and listing whole teams in project publicity and announcements of success— can improve coordination and interdependence within groups as well as the quality of the group process. The heroic individual mode of operation is much more aligned with male needs and norms than with female preferences. In fact, women looking at the same processes in which men see an individual contributor often notice other contributors who are not being recognized but without whom the project would have failed. Many women—and some men—prefer working in partnerships and teams and claiming less individual credit for their accomplishments. Organizations tend to expect and reward individual accomplishments even though they increasingly need team-based performance.

Some types of organizational culture find it harder than others to support team reward systems. In a hierarchical organization with a highly individualistic culture, a team-based reward system is likely to meet with considerable resistance. For such a structure to work, the culture needs to change to focus on participation, teamwork, and cohesiveness. In most organizations, team-based rewards are instituted as a supplement to existing compensation systems that continue to reward individuals based on what is seen as their personal merit, skills, and performance. Training may be necessary to teach managers as well as employees how to operate in the new environment.

Practices that support active work-life balance promote connection and intimacy as well as wholeness. For example, managers who take advantage of flexible work arrangements can reconfigure their schedules to allow them to be with their families while the children are awake and need their attention. Among the women in our study, we saw such benefits used to make more time to reconnect with elderly parents, husbands, and friends. All these efforts allowed greater satisfaction of the desire to connect intimately with others.

Agency

Like connection, agency—the desire to control one's destiny—is one of the strongest human needs. Agency has stereotypically been associated with men, who are seen as the embodiment of assertive, goal-driven, agentic behavior, and organizations have been structured to nurture that drive in men. In *Beyond Ambition* (1991), Robert Kaplan and his colleagues argue that organizational culture is so efficient at stimulating the development of agency in male executives that the executives lose sight of their desires for connection. The norms of competition, dominance, and individual achievement sustain the male drive for agency.

The story with women is much more complex. Like men, women managers work in environments that emphasize achievement and goal accomplishment. However, organizations send different messages to men and women, giving men much more latitude. Men can use a variety of command-and-control, persuasive, and risk-taking techniques, whereas gender stereotypes hold women to a more limited range. As discussed in Chapter Three, many behaviors admired in men evoke criticism—too aggressive, too strong, too macho—in women. But if women act too feminine, they are seen as too soft for the job. In *Breaking the Glass Ceiling*, Morrison, White, and Van Velsor (1992) describe this phenomenon as a *narrow band* of acceptable behavior that hampers women's ability to lead effectively. It is hard to shape your environment without a full kit of influence tools. Limiting women's agency limits their effectiveness on the job, so organizations need to reduce their reliance on stereotypes and learn what it really takes to perform well as a manager.

Meanwhile, it isn't enough to find and cling to the narrow band. Faced with new global challenges and increasing internal diversity, organizations are beginning to recognize and emphasize stereotypically feminine skills such as emotional intelligence and relational leadership. Sally Helgesen (1990) refers to these skills as the "female advantage." However, Joyce Fletcher (1999) points out that relational leadership gets "disappeared"—that is, this work goes unnoticed because others assume women engage in it because they enjoy it, not because the behaviors are particularly effective at work. Upon learning this, women often try to become what the organization seems to demand. They operate in traditionally masculine ways (toned down to fit within the narrow acceptable band), a choice that may well keep them from practicing the important, newly recognized relational leadership skills. The organization will be deprived of their abilities in these critical areas, and everyone will suffer as a result.

A second complicating factor in women's development of agency is blatant sexual harassment and discrimination. Controlling your destiny is exceptionally difficult when people are actively blocking you and punishing you for being female. Of course, organizations can be so generally abusive that it is hard for anyone to be agentic, but women managers are more likely than men to find themselves constrained by a harassing environment.

Sexual discrimination and harassment on the basis of gender are of course illegal. Organizations have policies to address these issues. The problem, however, is that despite all their policies, organizations still tolerate sexism and discrimination in various forms. To ensure that such policies are used and that there is zero tolerance for harassment or discrimination, senior managers must demonstrate visibly that such behaviors are unacceptable.

One woman worked at a company well known for its diversity initiatives, but she still felt harassed when she took a long maternity leave. Her boss and coworkers joked about her time off in front of senior managers, who did nothing. For real zero tolerance of gender discrimination, top management must act every time they hear comments against women, especially gender-based comments. It is incumbent on them to send the message to all levels of the organization that hostile comments are not acceptable. They need to recognize that sexual harassment doesn't have to be obvious and blunt to be detrimental. The subtle kind is deadly as well. Human resource departments and senior managers need to work together to see that harassment and discrimination are always recognized, noted, and censured.

In an in-depth look at ways to advance women, the Conference Board of Canada (Orser, 2001) strongly recommends that employees be held accountable for comments or behaviors that limit the careers of women. The group also makes the point that for women to succeed and achieve, senior management needs to be clearly behind them. They have found that executive commitment is the strongest factor encouraging the advancement of women. This seems only natural—agency involves demonstrating your own power, and that is obviously easier to do when others with power show their confidence in and commitment to your success. Men don't have this problem. They don't have to prove that people of their gender can be strong leaders. They don't need to be visibly reinforced for taking action. Women as a group can be more agentic if executive commitment to their advancement is visible.

Another practice that helps create a supportive environment is diversity training, which can make the organizational culture more open to both genders as well as to differences in race and ethnicity. Several companies have programs to help male managers adjust to the fact that their peer group now includes women. Deloitte & Touche has a well-known "Men and Women as Colleagues" program that deals with some of the complexities that arise when both genders work together. Programs such as these help change culture by surfacing the subtle ways that discrimination shows itself in organizational settings. They allow an open discussion of issues that once were taboo. The dialog about gender stimulates cultural change in gender relations. In Deloitte & Touche, nearly every manager has attended these workshops. According to an article in *Harvard Business Review,* these workshops have been pivotal events in understanding how gender has affected work climate in the organization (McCracken, 2000).

Discriminatory reward systems also hinder the development of agency in women. According to the U.S. Department of Labor, in the year 2000 women were paid only 68 percent as much as men in similar managerial positions. It is very difficult to feel agentic when you see somebody with a Y chromosome raking in more than you are for doing the same job. Therefore it is vital to address this issue on multiple levels. Human resource practitioners should review compensation practices and eliminate wage differentials for the same work. Top managers need to set the vision and the stage for this to happen—and then they must address gender inequities in pay. At all levels, women's immediate bosses need to ensure that compensation depends on work and performance, not sex.

Evaluation issues further complicate the effects of compensation on agency. To enhance agency, organizations should define *good performance* properly and avoid confusing "face time" with work time. Organizations that ask managers and professionals to work sixty- or seventy-hour weeks (or more) often assume that more hours at the office equal more performance. But boosting face time not only fails to boost productivity, it puts people with caregiving responsibilities in particularly tenuous situations and damages all employees' work-life balance. Organizations should focus performance evaluation on what actually gets done.

Similarly, performance criteria could include all the work the organization wants to encourage. A number of women told us about work they did building teams and developing relationships that went unacknowledged, echoing Fletcher's observation that relationship management in organizations is often invisible at evaluation and reward time. This activity is vital to performance and is work that women tend to take on to keep teams committed and moving. This form of agency—the active fostering of productive relationships—is difficult to maintain when no one notices or pays for it.

We urge organizations to take a good look at their performance evaluation systems. Again, this is a place where top managers can influence the organization's mind-set. We urge executives to make sure their organizations are using appropriate selection and promotion criteria, and are looking at what really matters for performance—not just at the range of task-related skills associated with the stereotypical male manager. Definitions of agency and leadership behaviors should be broadened to include initiating and maintaining key relationships, managing conflict productively, fostering high morale in teams, and other relationship tasks.

Promotion and selection decisions are also influenced by the visibility of various candidates. Visibility leads to greater opportunity, and greater opportunity leads to rewards that include still greater visibility and the learning and growth that come with experience. Women who are agentic or want to become more agentic want opportunities to achieve. Practices that enhance their visibility help women get both the rewards associated with agency and more opportunities to develop agency. For example, at Allstate the succession-planning process is orchestrated to ensure that a diverse set of candidates is developed for each position. Positions key to the company's strategy are identified nationwide, and potential candidates are monitored by race and gender as well as by performance. An affirmative action analysis against diversity goals for each business is considered before an appointment is made (Allstate, 1997). For women to develop agentically, they need access to the same high-impact opportunities that men have.

Some of the most important influences on an organization's developmental climate for women happen at the level of the work group. When asked what advice they would give corporate America regarding the development of women managers, women most often responded, "Treat us with respect." They went on to explain that being able to take significant action is much easier in an environment that respects its employees. We heard of many instances of lack of respect—men stole women's ideas, talked over women in meetings, and ignored women's concerns and contributions. To grow and develop agentically, women must be given credit and listened to. It is difficult to feel agentic if your ideas are continually claimed by others or overlooked. Norms of work groups and interpersonal relationships need to change to create a performance culture inclusive of women.

Self-Clarity

A woman who is high in self-clarity is aware of not only her strengths, weaknesses, preferences, and styles but also of her environment's influences on her behavior. She understands the norms of her organization and how well they fit with her needs. She sees herself objectively and can discern what she is responsible for and what is caused by the situation. Self-clarity helps improve strengths, shore up weaknesses, find reinforcing situations, and navigate in difficult environments. Organizations often have roadblocks that obstruct the development of self-clarity—feedback-poor environments and procedures that obscure what gender is and is not affecting in the workplace.

One of the most important steps to help women (and men) develop self-clarity is to offer supportive, constructive, and accurate feedback. Feedback can be delivered in three ways: through informal day-to-day conversations relevant to the conduct of work, through administrative reviews designed to produce performance documentation and decide pay, and through developmental reviews designed to stimulate behavior change and guide development planning. *Informal feedback* refers to the everyday coaching that takes place among colleagues. *Administrative feedback* often groups people into broad performance categories for salary or bonus determination. *Developmental feedback* is usually much more detailed and is intended to help managers achieve their personal potential. It often takes the form of feedback on multirater instruments, sometimes called 360-degree feedback. All three are important for self-clarity and are common in Fortune 1000 organizations—but they are rarely done well.

Carefully given feedback can build self-clarity. Poorly given feedback can reduce it—and our interviews were rife with reports of incompetent feedback. Organizations pay attention to the mechanics of performance feedback when what they really need is attention to the *process* of how feedback is delivered. To enhance self-clarity, feedback must be as specific, accurate, and helpful as possible. That means the recipient must accept the data—something most likely to happen if the feedback is delivered in a psychologically safe environment and if it comes from someone the recipient respects and trusts.

Human resource specialists can and should train managers and executives to give and receive feedback in a way that is psychologically safe and likely to be seen as accurate and honest. This process can go awry if the feedback is shaped by prejudice and bias or if appropriate and necessary feedback is perceived by the recipient as an attack. Executives and managers who give feedback should remember that people will naturally try to figure out if prejudice or discrimination has influenced what they're hearing. Very simply, people have a tough time learning from feedback if they believe prejudice is involved, so giving feedback that is of high quality and as free from bias as possible is critical. At the same time, the feedback giver's fear that justifiable negative feedback will be misperceived as prejudice adds another complication to the feedback process. These complexities make it doubly important for executives and managers to understand the nuances of giving feedback.

Top management plays a key role in creating a climate that supports the delivery of quality feedback. Senior managers could model in clear ways with their direct reports that they take feedback processes seriously. Training on the delivery of feedback is amply available and top managers should visibly take part in it. They can also demonstrate that they value feedback by asking their staff for it, responding to it respectfully, and making appropriate changes in their own behavior.

At the work-group level, frontline managers can follow and model the human resource practices that deal with feedback delivery. Like managers at all levels, they need to take advantage of programs that help them give and receive honest feedback, and to ask for and learn from feedback from their own associates. They share the responsibility for creating a climate in which it is safe to deliver and receive feedback.

Self-clarity involves much more than the delivery and receipt of feedback; it also involves understanding the environment. The employee groups described in the section on enhancing connection are one way to help women managers make sense of their environment, allowing them to get together to talk over the climate for women managers in their organization, profession, or industry. This can be a big help in figuring out how much others' perceptions of their actions and behaviors are influenced by the way women in general are treated in that setting.

In terms of helping women understand the general environment, senior managers can help develop their subordinates' self-clarity by openly communicating business priorities and concerns. To understand yourself, you have to understand your situation. Senior managers who share as much contextual information as possible—knowledge of business concerns, competitor activities, pending legal issues, and strategic issues can help people (regardless of gender) see how they fit into the larger picture. Some of the managers in our study were in danger of taking situations too personally because they did not understand the surrounding organizational dynamics. When they hunted for the relevant information, they realized that aspects of a troubling situation were endemic to the organization or the industry, and that knowledge let them respond more appropriately. For these women, it would have been helpful if the ongoing flow of information about the environment was richer and more accessible. This same issue is important at the work-group level as well. Frontline managers can help by being as honest and open as possible in their communications with their staff.

Other Considerations

Organizational change is more than just introducing basic programs and initiatives. To make implementation of such strategies effective, people in an organization need a business case that justifies the effort. They should also understand that there's no such thing as a quick fix in this area, and that even a program that works will endure only if it is built into the organization's basic structure. Exhibit 7.1 summarizes the actions to be taken.

EXHIBIT 7.1. A Developmental Thumbnail for What Companies Can Do.

1. Build support.
   - Frame gender diversity as a business advantage.
   - Assess how well your organization is doing at retaining and developing women managers.
2. Give it time to work.
   - Implement practices to support the development of authenticity, agency, connection, wholeness, and self-clarity.
   - Experiment with different practices.
   - Reward practices that enhance these dimensions, not just those that satisfy traditionally male norms.
   - Support culture change at all levels of the organization, from top management to work group.
   - Continually assess and reward progress.
3. Institutionalize change.

Building Support

First, you can convince your organization to move in the direction outlined in this chapter if you can make a business case for diversity. This process has two parts: convincing your organization that diversity is good for business, and demonstrating your organization's current level of retention and development of women managers. You may find it useful to discuss these competitive advantages (based on Cox and Blake, 1991):

- Diversity is a feature of the changing marketplace. It is in an organization's best interest to have a human resource mix reflecting the target market.

- Creativity and innovation can be enhanced through the variety of views and opinions available. The perspectives of a diverse group can stimulate a broader selection of ideas and approaches.

- Diversity of perspectives can stimulate better problem solving and decision making. Organizations today face many complex challenges; having more perspectives means having more options and making better decisions.

- Acceptance of diversity helps prepare an organization to deal with other types of change. This is important during these rapidly changing times.

These four generic reasons can be tailored to reflect the specific strategic issues in your organization. Try weaving them into the goals outlined in the corporate strategy and the challenges facing your organization.

In developing a business case, it also helps to look at indicators of women's acceptance in the organizational culture. There is nothing like good data to make a point. Consider what indicators of women's progress are central in your setting. You may want to include the following: turnover rates, promotion rates, utilization of flexible work arrangements, lawsuits, complaints or grievances, and representation of women in succession plans, high-visibility jobs, mentoring programs, career planning systems, and formal training activities. These indicators can show how well (or how badly) your organization is doing with regard to encouraging and recognizing women managers. The numbers can be used to get the attention of top management and can create a powerful incentive for change.

Once the business case for cultural change is made, be sure to assess and reward progress as it occurs. The indicators used in making a business case for diversity can also serve as indicators of progress. Organizations can hold senior managers accountable for diversity by linking progress on these indicators to executive compensation. Companies such as Deloitte & Touche regularly review the representation of women in high-impact assignments. During the annual business planning process, they also set goals for their human resource and women managers' initiatives (Trimberger, 1998). Leaders are held responsible for continuous progress toward these goals, and performance ratings and compensation are tied to their results. Deloitte & Touche carefully monitors its benchmarks of promotion and turnover rates for women, admission to partnership, use of flexible work arrangements, and human resource standards (Deloitte & Touche, 2001). The company also uses an external advisory committee to help monitor progress toward these goals.

Settling In for the Long Haul

Culture change is never a quick fix. Changing the business culture to represent a wide range of human values will take a long-term commitment. Too often we hear of organizations trying out work-life policies or diversity initiatives and abandoning them because change did not happen quickly. Don't expect rapid change. Implementing a cultural change that will endure takes a long time. Adults don't learn new behaviors quickly and easily—they need time to adjust to different norms and expectations. Communicate the changes and goals repeatedly and in a variety of ways.

Experiment with different models of introducing change into the system to see what works most effectively. Any of a wide range of practices and policies can help move an organization toward a more woman-friendly culture. It's necessary to see what works in a given setting and customize the approach to fit the situation. Borrowing another organization's plan is not likely to meet your needs. Changes can be dramatic and large, shortening the transition period but increasing the stress of the change period, or they can be gradual and incremental, lessening the shock but risking the discontent of employees because the changes take so long (Ely & Meyerson, 1999).

Consolidating Change

Finally, any change that is effective needs to be institutionalized. One person cannot stand as the model for change or as the symbol of it. In one company we worked with, for example, a diversity initiative foundered for lack of widespread support. One member of the executive team, a white male, fought for the initiative and stood as its champion. Others saw it as his issue and did not take it seriously—even the women on the executive team ignored it. One of the few women on the team attended a company-sponsored conference for women. She left the session early and discarded her name tag in front of the other conference attendees. Her behavior spoke volumes: attending to women was not an important value to her. The advocate left felt trapped. Unless change is institutionalized and owned by many, it is very difficult to make it stick. From the beginning and throughout the process, the executive team as a whole has responsibility for changing the culture.

Parting Thoughts

Some of our key points bear reiteration. Organizations are at a critical juncture with regard to women. It's becoming clear that it pays to consider women as part of the talent pool, and organizations are hiring more and more of them. Women are in the executive pipeline—but they're not moving up it either quickly or smoothly. In fact, once in the pipeline, many are electing to drop out again. They go off on their own to escape the assumption that all managerial employees must subscribe to a set of male norms and standards—a set of norms that is outdated today by any perspective, female or male. It is vital for organizations to actively respect the unique needs and contributions of women. They no longer want to be seen as exceptions to the norm, and organizations will profit by encouraging and developing women as part of the norm rather than as exceptions.

The developmental journeys of managerial women reflect five fundamental themes—authenticity, connection, agency, wholeness, and self-clarity—all of which influence much of adult life and development. All five are as valid for men as for women, though women speak more openly and freely about them. In this book we talk about how they play out for women managers at this time in the United States. They are experiencing more freedom and opportunity than ever before and organizations are realizing they must change the ways in which they operate in order to retain talented women. These themes shape the contours of the life choices and trade-offs of women managers. They influence personal decisions about what opportunities to take, skip, trade off, modify, and create.

The work we have started here looks only at one group of managerial women—those who happened to join a particular CCL program, and who chose to participate in the study. This sample was largely white and entirely based in the United States. It would be useful to look at these themes in other samples of women to see how they play out in other countries and ethnic groups. Audience responses from diverse groups of women suggest the issues are widely relevant, but the nuances may differ. For example, when we shared our findings with a group of Frenchwomen, they told us they experienced some wholeness issues differently because their country has a different systemic approach to child care. African American women told us of greater obstacles to overcome in terms of being agentic than those reported by the white women. Particular legal issues, societal customs, historical events, and stereotypes influence how these issues may reveal themselves. The constant, we expect, is that these five themes guide both development and life choices. Given the increasing demand for leadership talent, organizations cannot afford to misunderstand the career and life needs of any group of potential stars. We urge others to investigate and attempt to understand the needs of a wider group of women so that organizations can modify their development approaches to be more inclusive in their search for the leaders they need.

Finally, we urge organizations to take advantage of the new wave of talent coming their way. Women present a formidable force. Moving them from the managerial to the executive pipeline can keep American organizations at the forefront of the global marketplace. Let's not waste the opportunity.

Appendix: The Research Design

This study was designed to assess the factors that have influenced the lives and choices of women who were in upper levels of management at the end of the twentieth century, so as to provide assistance and insight for those approaching or at those levels in the opening years of the twenty-first. It began with 61 volunteers who were extensively interviewed and most of the work was with them, but was later expanded to include survey questions addressed to 276 women of similar background.

The Study Participants

The interviewees in our study were all high-achieving women with careers in middle or senior management. They ranged in age from twenty-six to fifty-eight, with an average age of forty. Seventy-one percent were married and involved in a committed relationship and half had children under the age of eighteen. They were extremely well educated, with 92 percent having bachelor's degrees and 51 percent having a graduate degree as well. The sample was limited in terms of race, with 92 percent being white.

The Program

The women in this study attended The Women's Leadership Program (TWLP) at CCL in 1995 and 1996. The program, which draws managers from all over the United States and occasionally from other countries, emphasizes assessment for purposes of development. Prior to attending the workshop, the women complete a variety of inventories including tests of personality, preferences, and 360-degree performance evaluations. The program provides feedback on these inventories woven into content about effective leadership and the leadership development process, and culminates in a private session with a feedback coach who focuses on helping integrate the results of the different assessments. The women are challenged to try out new leadership behaviors in the workshop's supportive environment. For many women this is the first time they have had a real peer group from whom to seek advice and support. Throughout the program, participants have opportunities to reflect and to set goals. Although the program emphasizes leadership behavior, leadership is presented in the context of the whole life.

The Study Design

The study was designed to develop our understanding of the questions and issues high-achieving women face in defining and shaping their careers. We asked these women to share with us one year of their life journey via three interviews: just after the program, six months later, and a year after the program. In each interview, we asked the women what issues were salient to them, what kind of progress they were making on their goals, if any changes had occurred in their life, and what type of obstacles they were encountering in their careers. Questions were designed to elicit both a sense of the struggles the women were experiencing and the steps they were taking in response.

Besides the women themselves, we also interviewed the feedback coaches from the program, who helped us identify the key issues facing each manager. The coaches provided an additional perspective on each individual's level of insight as well as a professional lens through which to understand her struggles. The issues explored in each interview are listed in Exhibit A.1 at the end

of this Appendix, and the actual interview protocols are available on the Jossey-Bass Web site. These women gave us their permission to use their stories in service of our research. In this book you read of their trials, tribulations, and victories. Each example shared in the book is actually a composite of several individuals who shared a common experience. All examples disguise the identity of the participants.

Finding the Themes

We used an inductive approach to identify the themes. That is, we started this study without a hypothesis about what we wanted to find, and allowed the themes to emerge from the data. This approach is called *grounded theory* (Glaser & Strauss, 1967). Essentially we reviewed the data many, many times in different ways looking for salient themes in the data.

Our first step was to tape and transcribe the initial interviews. At least two people read each interview and discussed it in depth. We developed a case summary document for each woman based on our understanding of the interviews and assessment data. Before the second interview we prepared customized follow-up questions based on the individual situation. Then we followed the same process of transcribing the interview, discussing it, and developing the case summary. We used a similar process for the third and final interview. The final case summary for each woman contained a section on her background, a review of her coach's comments, a chronology of events that occurred during the year, a summary of current issues in her life, a summary of her expressed goals, and a summary of the steps she took to reach both her directly expressed and less directly expressed goals.

Our next step was to identify patterns in the data. As we conducted the interviews we systematically discussed them and noted our developing conclusions. We used the case summaries to identify themes in the data. Each case was put together with a random group of four others and was compared and contrasted with the

other cases by a group of two to four researchers. The themes of wholeness, agency, and connection dominated both the interviews and our discussions of them. The themes of authenticity and self-clarity were subtler but emerged as we went along, and by the end we saw very clear patterns regarding the nature of each of the five themes. At times we considered combining authenticity and wholeness because of their substantial conceptual overlap. We also considered combining authenticity and self-clarity. We decided, however, to leave them as distinct since their differences were quite salient.

Refining the Themes

We took several steps to refine the themes, reviewing all the cases and identifying five to ten women who were high and the same number who were low on each theme. The cases for the groups were compared and contrasted so that factors differentiating the two groups could be identified. We developed an understanding of each theme based on these factors and documented the understanding in a codebook. Focusing on each theme separately, one or the other of us then reviewed all the cases in light of that theme to develop her understanding of the material and reported this in an internal memo. Finally, we checked our conclusions by asking two of our colleagues to independently go through a subset of eighteen cases on a theme-by-theme basis and code the cases for evidence of the themes. These colleagues helped us challenge our thinking and pushed us to refine our understanding of the phenomena.

Looking for Effectiveness

In addition to understanding what themes were most prevalent in the interviews, we also wanted to see how they were related to performance. To do this, we identified the women who were performing unusually well or unusually poorly in the eyes of their coworkers.

From TWLP, we had access to performance ratings provided by bosses, peers, and direct reports. We took the average of these ratings and identified the women at the extremes: the nine who were one standard deviation or more above the mean and the nine who were one standard deviation or more below it. Then we compared the interview summaries for each group and looked for commonalities—that is, we looked for what the most effective women had in common with each other and then separately we looked for what the least effective women had in common. Next we compared what we knew about the two groups and identified themes that differentiated them, finding that the distinguishing skills and outlooks on life were those that governed the way the women addressed their concerns with authenticity, agency, connection, wholeness, and self-clarity.

Furthermore, we found a new factor that was important, organizational climate. Women others saw as performing well described their organizations as supportive of development in general and women in particular. Women others saw as performing poorly described their organizations as unsupportive of women and tolerant of harassment and discrimination. Such problems could be the source of the poor performance, but we have no way of knowing what came first, the climate or the performance. This led us to conclude that organizational climate plays a key role in understanding leadership effectiveness for women. Focusing simply on individual actions and behaviors is insufficient.

Looking for Age Differences

To understand age differences, we sorted the women into five age groups: 29–33, 34–40, 41–45, 46–50, and 51–55. There were too few women below age 29 or above 55 to analyze them for age differences. We were interested in learning if different themes were more salient for women of different ages. In our first pass, we reviewed the case summaries in each age group and wrote memos describing common issues. We then compared the women from the various age groups to identify contrasts between the groups. The findings were summarized in an internal memo. In a second step, we identified a subset of three women in each group and asked a research assistant to review these fifteen cases to see if any new age-related themes above and beyond the five primaries could be detected. The assistant noticed that women's approach to goal attainment varied by age group, but we decided not to include this as a separate theme in this study since the goal attainment perspective overlapped substantially with the theme of agency.

Expanding the Study

We were very intrigued by the comments the women made in the initial interviews about the theme of wholeness. The desire to feel whole and to fit one's work comfortably in the context of a whole life seemed to be such a paramount desire of these women that we expanded the study to include more managers and to look at this issue in more depth. To that end, we conducted a survey of 276 additional women, with measures of tenure, career history, family configuration, life satisfaction, career satisfaction, global self-esteem, organization-based self-esteem, commitment to different life roles, and organizational climate for women. Some of the items on this survey were developed specifically for this research; most were taken from previously validated scales. A copy of the full survey is available on the Jossey-Bass Web site. These women were also participants in TWLP but did not take part in the interviews. We asked for and got their permission to look at their assessment data from the program, which included the California Psychological Inventory (CPI; Gough & Bradley, 1996) and ratings of the effectiveness of their leadership skills from superiors, subordinates, and peers in their home organization. Leadership effectiveness was assessed via a 360-degree survey instrument developed by the Clark Wilson Group.

Based on responses to the initial interviews and the emphasis on wholeness in these interviews, we focused on the experiences of women who had many life roles. These women told us they paid a price in terms of not feeling whole, but they also described many benefits of a multiple-role lifestyle. We were intrigued by this and wanted to see if there were positive outcomes associated with multiple roles. We found that a varied life (for example, being a mother, partner, friend, or volunteer as well as a manager) was positively related to features of well-being such as life satisfaction (as measured by Diener, Emmons, Larsen, & Griffin, 1985) and self-acceptance as measured on the CPI. Further, and perhaps more striking, a life with multiple roles was positively related to interpersonal and task-related managerial skills as assessed via the 360-degree feedback. We concluded that although having a life outside work causes many conflicts, it also brings benefits that have an impact at work as well. The full report of this study, based on many different analyses, is in Ruderman, Ohlott, Panzer, and King (2002), available from the authors.

EXHIBIT A.1. Topics Explored in the Interviews.

The Initial Interview

- Key life choices
- Current major concerns, issues, or transitions
- Definitions of success and fulfillment
- Relationships between personal and private spheres of life
- Hopes and fears for the next year
- Goals for the next year

The Six-Month Follow-Up Interview

- Life update (family issues, personal issues, disruptions, key decisions, changes, new realizations, struggles, sources of stress)
- Clarification of issues from the first interview
- Customized questions following up on individual issues, choices, transitions, and goals

- Trade-offs and compromises
- Anticipated changes for the future

The One-Year Follow-Up Interview

- Life update
- Reflections on growth over the year
- Reevaluation of hopes and fears acknowledged in the initial interview
- Customized questions following up on individual issues, choices, transitions, and goals
- Clarification of issues from the six-month interview
- Advice to other women, advice to corporate America
- Perspectives on earlier choices or trade-offs

The Feedback Coach Interview

- General impressions of the participant based on assessment data
- Key issues in participant's life (dilemmas, transitions, obstacles)
- Assessment of self-awareness
- Comparison to other participants in terms of salient life issues

References

Acker, J. (1998). Hierarchies, jobs, bodies: A theory of gendered organizations. In K. A. Myers, C. D. Anderson, & B. J. Risman (Eds.), *Feminist foundations: Toward transforming sociology* (pp. 299–317). Thousand Oaks, CA: Sage.

Allstate. (1997, January). 1997 Catalyst award winners at diversity forefront. Available online: http://147.208.7.140/Media/news/pr_1997/ pr_7jan97.html. Access date January 28, 2002.

Bakan, D. (1966). *The duality of human existence*. Boston: Beacon Press.

Ban Breathnach, S. (1995). *Simple abundance: A daybook of comfort and joy*. New York: Warner Books.

Ban Breathnach, S. (1998). *Something more: Excavating your authentic self*. New York: Warner Books.

Barnett, R. C., & Hyde, J. S. (2001). Women, men, work, and family. *American Psychologist, 56*(10), 781–796.

Barnett, R. C., & Marshall, N. L. (1993). Men, family-role quality, job-role quality, and physical health. *Health Psychology, 12*, 48–55.

Beatty, C. A. (1996). The stress of managerial and professional women: Is the price too high? *Journal of Organizational Behavior, 17*, 233–251.

Belenky, M. F., Clinchy, B. M., Goldberger, N. R., & Tarule, J. M. (1986). *Women's ways of knowing: The development of self, voice and mind*. New York: Basic Books.

Byalick, M., & Saslow, L. (1995). *How come I feel so disconnected if this is such a user-friendly world?* Princeton, NJ: Peterson's.

Catalyst. (1996). *Women in corporate leadership: Progress and prospects*. New York: Author.

Catalyst. (2000). *Catalyst census of women corporate officers and top earn-ers*. New York: Author.

Church, A. H. (1997). Managerial self-awareness in high-performing individuals in organizations. *Journal of Applied Psychology, 82*(2), 281–292.

Cox, T., Jr. (1994). *Cultural diversity in organizations: Theory, research and practice*. San Francisco: Berrett-Koehler.

Cox, T. H., Jr., & Blake, S. (1991). Managing cultural diversity: Impli-cations for organizational competitiveness. *Executive, 5*(3), 45–56.

Crosby, F. J., & Jaskar, K. L. (1993). Women and men at home and at work: Realities and illusions. In S. Oskamp & M. Costanzo (Eds.), *Gender issues in contemporary society* (pp. 143–171). Thousand Oaks, CA: Sage.

Deloitte & Touche. (2001). Women's initiative. Available online: http:// www.us.deloitte.com/Women. Access date December 14, 2001.

Diener, E., Emmons, R. A., Larsen, R. J., & Griffin, S. (1985). The sat-isfaction with life scale. *Journal of Personality Assessment, 49*, 71–75.

Dutton, G. (1998, September). Cutting-edge stressbusters. *HR Focus, 75*(9), 11–12.

Ely, R. J. (1994). The effects of organizational demographics and social identity on relationships among professional women. *Administrative Science Quarterly, 39*(2), 203–238.

Ely, R. J., & Meyerson, D. E. (1999, Spring). Moving from gender to di-versity in organizational diagnosis and intervention. *Diversity Fac-tor*, pp. 28–33.

Engoron, F. (1997, August). Price Waterhouse: Initiatives for retaining women. *HR Focus, 74*(8), 9–10.

Families and Work Institute. (1997). *The 1997 national study of the chang-ing workforce*. New York: Author.

Fletcher, J. K. (1999). *Disappearing acts: Gender, power, and relational practice at work*. Cambridge, MA: MIT Press.

Fredrickson, B. L. (2001). The role of positive emotions in positive psy-chology: The broaden-and-build theory of positive emotions. *Amer-ican Psychologist, 56*(3), 218–226.

Friedan, B. (1963). *The feminine mystique*. London: Penguin.

Gilligan, C. (1982). *In a different voice: Psychological theory and women's development*. Cambridge, MA: Harvard University Press.

Glaser, B. G., & Strauss, A. L. (1967). *The discovery of grounded theory.* Chicago: Aldine.

Goleman, D. (1998). *Working with emotional intelligence.* New York: Bantam.

Gough, H. G., & Bradley, P. (1996). *California Psychological Inventory.* Palo Alto, CA: Consulting Psychologists Press.

Graham, B. W. (1996). The business argument for flexibility. *HR Magazine, 41*(5), 104–109.

Griffith, P. G., MacBride-King, J. L., & Townsend, B. (1998). *Closing the gap: Women's advancement in corporate and professional Canada.* Ottawa: Conference Board of Canada & Catalyst.

Grover, M. B. (1999, September 6). Daddy stress. *Forbes,* pp. 202–208.

Helgesen, S. (1990). *The female advantage: Women's ways of leadership.* New York: Doubleday.

Helgeson, V. S. (1994). Relation of agency and communion to well-being: Evidence and potential explanations. *Psychological Bulletin, 116*(3), 412–428.

Helgeson, V. S., & Fritz, H. L. (2000). The implications of unmitigated agency and unmitigated communion for domains of problem behavior. *Journal of Personality, 68*(6), 1031–1057.

Helson, R. (1997). The self in middle age. In M. E. Lachman & J. B. James (Eds.), *Multiple paths of midlife development* (pp. 21–43). Chicago: University of Chicago Press.

Helson, R., & Moane, G. (1987). Personality change in women from college to midlife. *Journal of Personality and Social Psychology, 53,* 176–186.

Jamison, K. (1984). *The nibble theory and the kernel of power.* Mahwah, NJ: Paulist Press.

Jordan, J., Kaplan, A. G., Miller, J. B., Stiver, I. P., & Surrey, J. L. (1991). *Women's growth in connection: Writings from the Stone Center.* New York: Guilford Press.

Josselson, R. (1996). *The space between us: Exporing the dimensions of human relationships.* Thousand Oaks, CA: Sage.

Jung, C. G. (1950). *Modern man in search of a soul* (W. S. Dell and Cary F. Baynes, Trans.). New York: Harcourt. (Original work published 1933).

Kaplan, R. E., Drath, W. H., & Kofodimos, J. R. (1991). *Beyond ambition: How driven managers can lead better and live better*. San Francisco: Jossey-Bass.

Kegan, R. (1994). *In over our heads: The mental demands of modern life*. Cambridge, MA: Harvard University Press.

Kofodimos, J. R. (1993). *Balancing act: How managers can integrate successful careers and fulfilling personal lives*. San Francisco: Jossey-Bass.

Kram, K. E. (1988). *Mentoring at work: Developmental relationships in organizational life*. Lanham, MD: University Press of America.

Lee, R. J., & King, S. N. (2001). *Discovering the leader in you: A guide to realizing your personal leadership potential*. San Francisco: Jossey-Bass.

Lennick, D. (1999, September). *Leveraging your emotional competence*. Paper presented at the Emotional Intelligence Conference, Chicago, IL.

Leslie, J. B., & Van Velsor, E. (1996). *A look at derailment today: North America and Europe*. Greensboro, NC: Center for Creative Leadership.

Levinson, D. J. (1978). *The seasons of a man's life*. New York: Knopf.

Levinson, D. J. (1996). *The seasons of a woman's life*. New York: Knopf.

Mainiero, L. A. (1994). On breaking the glass ceiling: The political seasoning of powerful women executives. *Organizational Dynamics, 22*(4), 4–20.

Marks, S. R. (1977). Multiple roles and role strain: Some notes on human energy, time, and commitment. *American Sociological Review, 42,* 921–936.

McCracken, D. M. (2000). Winning the talent war for women: Sometimes it takes a revolution. *Harvard Business Review, 78*(6), 159–167.

McGuire, G. (1999). Race, sex, and corporate membership. In A. J. Murrell, F. J. Crosby, & R. J. Ely (Eds.), *Mentoring dilemmas: Developmental relationships within multicultural organizations* (pp. 105–120). Mahwah, NJ: Erlbaum.

McKenna, E. P. (1997). *When work doesn't work anymore: Women, work and identity*. New York: Bantam Doubleday.

Meyerson, D. E. (2001). *Tempered radicals: How people use difference to inspire change at work*. Boston: Harvard Business School Press.

Meyerson, D. E., & Fletcher, J. (2000). A modest manifesto for shattering the glass ceiling. *Harvard Business Review, 78*(1), 126–136.

Miller, J. B. (1986). *Toward a new psychology of women* (2nd ed.). Boston: Beacon Press.

Miller, J. B., & Stiver, I. P. (1997). *The healing connection: How women form relationships in therapy and in life*. Boston: Beacon Press.

Moen, P., Dempster-McClain, D., & Williams, R. M. (1992). Successful aging: A life-course perspective on women's multiple roles and health. *American Journal of Sociology, 97*(6), 1612–1638.

Moore, D. P., & Buttner, E. H. (1997). *Women entrepreneurs: Moving beyond the glass ceiling*. Thousand Oaks, CA: Sage.

Morrison, A. M. (1992). *The new leaders: Guidelines on leadership diversity in America*. San Francisco: Jossey-Bass.

Morrison, A. M., White, R. P., & Van Velsor, E. (1992). *Breaking the glass ceiling: Can women reach the top of America's largest corporations?* (Updated ed.). Reading, MA: Addison-Wesley.

Orser, B. (2001). *Chief executive commitment: The key to enhancing women's advancement*. Ottawa: Conference Board of Canada.

Perlow, L. A. (1997). *Finding time: How corporations, individuals, and families can benefit from new work practices*. Ithaca, NY: ILR Press.

Potts, J. (1998). Metrics as mirror: Perception as reality. *Diversity Factor, 6*(3), 20–29.

Powell, G. N. (1999). Reflections on the glass ceiling. In G. N. Powell (Ed.), *Handbook of gender and work* (pp. 325–345). Thousand Oaks, CA: Sage.

Pulley, M. L. (1997). *Losing your job—Reclaiming your soul*. San Francisco: Jossey-Bass.

Putnam, R. D. (2000). *Bowling alone: The collapse and revival of American community*. New York: Simon & Schuster.

Quick, J. C., Gavin, J. H., Cooper, C. L., & Quick, J. D. (2000, May). Executive health: Building strength, managing risk. *Academy of Management Executive 14*(2), 34–44.

Rapoport, R., Bailyn, L., Fletcher, J. K., & Pruitt, B. H. (2002). *Beyond work-family balance: Advancing gender equity and workplace performance*. San Francisco: Jossey-Bass.

Ruderman, M. N., & Ohlott, P. J. (1994). *The realities of management promotion*. Greensboro, NC: Center for Creative Leadership.

Ruderman, M. N., Ohlott, P. J., Panzer, K., & King, S. N. (2002). Benefits of multiple roles for managerial women. *Academy of Management Journal, 45*(2).

Shalit, R. (2001, August). The taming of the shrews. *Elle*, pp. 102–104, 108–109, 200.

Sharpe, R. (2000, November 20). As leaders, women rule. *Business Week*, pp. 75–84.

Sieber, S. D. (1974). Toward a theory of role accumulation. *American Sociological Review, 39,* 567–578.

Society for Human Resource Management (SHRM) (2001, May 9). What is the "business case for diversity"? Available online: http://www.shrm.org/diversity/businesscase.htm. Access date January 28, 2002.

Staff. (2001, January). The business case for diversity. Available online: http://www.diversityinc.com/index.cfm?CFID=18349&CFTOKEN=8994177.j. Access date January 28, 2002.

Still, L. V. (1993). *Where to from here? The managerial woman in transition.* Sydney, Australia: Business & Professional Publishing.

Stogdill, R. C., & Coons, A. E. (1957). *Leader behavior: Its description and measurement* (Research Monograph No. 88). Columbus: Ohio State University.

Thomas, D. A., & Ely, R. J. (1996). Making differences matter: A new paradigm for managing diversity. *Harvard Business Review, 74*(5), 72–90.

Tornow, W. W., London, M., & CCL Associates. (1998). *Maximizing the value of 360-degree feedback: A process for successful individual and organizational development.* San Francisco: Jossey-Bass.

Trimberger, L. (1998, November). Deloitte & Touche: Retaining women means success. *HR Focus*, pp. 7–8.

U.S. Census Bureau. (1999). *Statistical abstract of the United States.* Washington, DC: U.S. Department of Commerce.

U.S. Department of Labor, Bureau of Labor Statistics. (2001). Highlights of women's earnings in 2000. Available online: http://stats.bls.gov/cps/cpswom2000.pdf. Access date January 28, 2002.

Whyte, W. F., Jr. (1956). *The organization man.* Garden City, NY: Anchor Books.

Williams, J. (2000). *Unbending gender: Why family and work conflict and what to do about it.* New York: Oxford University Press.

Wuthnow, R. (1998). *Loose connections: Joining together in America's fragmented communities.* Cambridge, MA: Harvard University Press.

Index

Research study, 4–5, 217–224; age differences examined in, 221–222; design of, 218–219; finding and refining themes in, 219–220; finding factors affecting performance in, 220–221; interviews conducted for, 5, 222–224; participants in, 4–5, 217; and The Women's Leadership Program, 217–218

Resilience: connection as supporting, 42; as element of effective agency, 93–94

Restructuring your thoughts, 132–133

Retention, authenticity's relationship to, 18

Rewards, team-based, 202. *See also* Compensation

Risk taking: authenticity as requiring, 32–33; calculated, as element of effective agency, 89–90; developing agency through, 78

Robin (pseudonym), 149

Role accumulation, 115–116

Ruderman, M. N., 106, 113, 115, 223

Ruth (pseudonym), 158

S

Sabbaticals, 195

Samantha (pseudonym), 88–89, 91

Saslow, L., 69

Saying no, 130–131

Seasons of a Man's Life (Levinson), 164

Seasons of a Woman's Life (Levinson), 164

Self, holistic view of, 131–132

Self-awareness: distinction between self-clarity and, 136; as element of effective agency, 90–91; techniques for developing, 26–32

Self-clarity, 8–9, 136–159; characteristics of women with, 146–151; described, 136–137; as dominant theme for women aged 51–55, 177–178, 182; how to develop, 151–156; importance of, 137–139; issues with low levels of, 139–143; issues with moderate and high levels of, 144–146; obstacles to, 156–159; organizational practices to support, 208–210; and women aged 29–33, 167–168; and women aged 34–40, 170; and women aged 41–45, 172–173; and women aged 46–50, 175–176

Self-empowerment, 103

Self-evaluation, to develop self-clarity, 153

Self-reflection: to develop wholeness, 131; by effectively agentic women, 91

Senior executive interview, 107, 108

Setting boundaries, as element of wholeness, 130–131

Sexual harassment. *See* Harassment

Shalit, R., 85

Sharon (pseudonym), 58

Sharpe, R., 12

Sieber, S. D., 115

Simple Abundance (Breathnach), 30

Single focus, as technique for developing wholeness, 132–133

Slowing down, to develop connection, 66–67

Socialization: of age cohorts, 183; as obstacle to developing agency, 74, 105–106

Social skills, needed by managers, 44–45

Society for Human Resource Management (SHRM), 192, 193

Society for Women Engineers, 201

Something More: Excavating Your Authentic Self (Breathnach), 31

Sophie (pseudonym), 20

Sounding board, using others as, 57–58

Spirituality, wholeness promoted by, 131

Staff, 198

Still, L. V., 112

Stiver, I. P., 40, 57, 60, 74, 75, 78

Stogdill, R. C., 115

Strauss, A. L., 219

Stress: dealing with, by viewing events as interconnected, 148; workplace, multiple life roles as buffering, 114–115

Study. *See* Research study

Success, personal definition of, 25–26

Support: building, for organizational change, 211–213; connection as providing, 41–42; for development of authenticity, 33; lack of, at work, 45–47; of management for organizational change, 193–194; of management for work-life policies, 198–199; whole life offering benefit of, 119–120

Surrey, J. L., 40, 74

Susan (pseudonym), 72–73

T

Taking action. *See* Action

Tarule, J. M., 41

About the Center
for Creative Leadership

Founded in 1970, the Center for Creative Leadership® (CCL®) is one of the world's largest institutions focusing on disseminating practical leadership knowledge for individuals and organizations. CCL's mission of advancing the understanding, practice, and development of leadership for the benefit of society worldwide has led to international recognition of its portfolio of programs, assessments, and publications. They are regarded among the best offered by any institution anywhere. The portfolio is supported by CCL's five practice areas—Leadership for Complex Challenges, Leading in the Context of Difference, Individual Leader Development, Sustainable Leadership Capacity, and Team Development.

Funding is derived primarily from tuition, sales of products and publications, royalties, and fees for service. In addition, CCL also seeks grants and donations from foundations, corporations, and individuals in support of its educational mission.

Open-Enrollment Leadership Programs

CCL's open-enrollment leadership programs focus on individuals and may be used within the context of an organization's leadership development efforts. These programs help participants achieve specific developmental goals.

Agency

Like connection, agency—the desire to control one's destiny—is one of the strongest human needs. Agency has stereotypically been associated with men, who are seen as the embodiment of assertive, goal-driven, agentic behavior, and organizations have been structured to nurture that drive in men. In *Beyond Ambition* (1991), Robert Kaplan and his colleagues argue that organizational culture is so efficient at stimulating the development of agency in male executives that the executives lose sight of their desires for connection. The norms of competition, dominance, and individual achievement sustain the male drive for agency.

The story with women is much more complex. Like men, women managers work in environments that emphasize achievement and goal accomplishment. However, organizations send different messages to men and women, giving men much more latitude. Men can use a variety of command-and-control, persuasive, and risk-taking techniques, whereas gender stereotypes hold women to a more limited range. As discussed in Chapter Three, many behaviors admired in men evoke criticism—too aggressive, too strong, too macho—in women. But if women act too feminine, they are seen as too soft for the job. In *Breaking the Glass Ceiling*, Morrison, White, and Van Velsor (1992) describe this phenomenon as a *narrow band* of acceptable behavior that hampers women's ability to lead effectively. It is hard to shape your environment without a full kit of influence tools. Limiting women's agency limits their effectiveness on the job, so organizations need to reduce their reliance on stereotypes and learn what it really takes to perform well as a manager.

Meanwhile, it isn't enough to find and cling to the narrow band. Faced with new global challenges and increasing internal diversity, organizations are beginning to recognize and emphasize stereotypically feminine skills such as emotional intelligence and relational leadership. Sally Helgesen (1990) refers to these skills as the "female advantage." However, Joyce Fletcher (1999) points out that relational leadership gets "disappeared"—that is, this work goes unnoticed because others assume women engage in it because they enjoy it, not because the behaviors are particularly effective at work. Upon learning this, women often try to become what the organization seems to demand. They operate in traditionally masculine ways (toned down to fit within the narrow acceptable band), a choice that may well keep them from practicing the important, newly recognized relational leadership skills. The organization will be deprived of their abilities in these critical areas, and everyone will suffer as a result.

A second complicating factor in women's development of agency is blatant sexual harassment and discrimination. Controlling your destiny is exceptionally difficult when people are actively blocking you and punishing you for being female. Of course, organizations can be so generally abusive that it is hard for anyone to be agentic, but women managers are more likely than men to find themselves constrained by a harassing environment.

Sexual discrimination and harassment on the basis of gender are of course illegal. Organizations have policies to address these issues. The problem, however, is that despite all their policies, organizations still tolerate sexism and discrimination in various forms. To ensure that such policies are used and that there is zero tolerance for harassment or discrimination, senior managers must demonstrate visibly that such behaviors are unacceptable.

One woman worked at a company well known for its diversity initiatives, but she still felt harassed when she took a long maternity leave. Her boss and coworkers joked about her time off in front of senior managers, who did nothing. For real zero tolerance of gender discrimination, top management must act every time they hear comments against women, especially gender-based comments. It is incumbent on them to send the message to all levels of the organization that hostile comments are not acceptable. They need to recognize that sexual harassment doesn't have to be obvious and blunt to be detrimental. The subtle kind is deadly as well. Human resource departments and senior managers need to work together

- The *Leadership Development Program (LDP)®*, *Foundations of Leadership*, and *The Looking Glass Experience* enable growth through developing personal awareness of one's leadership style and through identifying key areas of strength and weakness.

- *The African-American Leadership Program* and *The Women's Leadership Program* combine personal awareness of one's leadership style with research-based insights to show how leadership is affected by race and gender issues.

- The *Leading Creatively* program helps to understand how business performance and individual effectiveness relate to creativity.

- *Leadership at the Peak* and *Developing the Strategic Leader* use simulations and assessments to gain knowledge about how to lead and inspire change and revitalization.

- *Leadership and High-Performance Teams* shows how to develop and lead teams, turning average performers into a highly effective work group.

- *Coaching for Results* affirms the value of one-on-one developmental assistance, showing how it can be used to enhance individual and organizational effectiveness.

In October 2001, for the second consecutive time, CCL was ranked #1 for Leadership in *BusinessWeek* magazine's Executive Education Special Report. And CCL was the only non-degree business school to appear in *BusinessWeek*'s top 20 providers of non-degree programs for executives. Please visit www.ccl.org/programs.

Custom-Designed Leadership Development Initiatives

On request, CCL can design and implement a leadership development initiative for your organization, designed specifically to meet its needs. Initiatives vary from redesigned versions of one of CCL's open-enrollment programs to unique events that build an organization from the ground up. Please visit www.ccl.org/custom.

Coaching

CCL has long understood the importance of honest, insightful, and confidential coaching in developing strong leaders. Our programs are distinct, and all include a reliance on quality assessment; rigorously trained coaches, ethics, and confidentiality; emphasis on the individual's development; and use of best practices throughout. For information on *Follow-on Coaching* (follows leadership programs), *Executive Coaching* (a venue for organizations that want a designed program without the classroom experience), and *Awareness Program for Executive Excellence (APEX)*® (for the most senior-level executives), please visit www.ccl.org/coaching.

Products

CCL pioneered the use of 360-degree assessment and feedback to help individuals, teams, and organizations learn about themselves. Assessments are an effective and necessary starting point for learning, growth, and change. Critical tools in both CCL and clients' development programs, they are also used on a stand-alone basis. CCL can provide facilitation services or train your trainers and facilitators in the use of these resources:

- *360 BY DESIGN*℠, a customizable, Internet-based 360-degree survey with on-line development planning and available support services.
- *Benchmarks*®, CCL's flagship 360-degree assessment tool that focuses on leadership skills and perspectives but also includes insights into potential flaws that can derail a career.
- *Prospector*®, for assessing ability to learn and willingness to take advantage of growth opportunities.

- *SKILLSCOPE®*, for assessing skills necessary for managerial effectiveness.

- *KEYS® to Creativity*, for organizations that want to enhance the environment for creativity and innovation.

    Please visit www.ccl.org/assessments.

Publications

Through its publications, CCL aims to improve the current understanding, practice, and development of leadership by disseminating the latest practical knowledge gained in the course of CCL's research and educational activities. In addition to copublishing books and a magazine with Jossey-Bass, a Wiley company, on a variety of leadership topics, CCL also publishes independently through CCL Press.

Of particular interest to many leaders is the CCL Press *Ideas Into Action Guidebook* series. Geared to the practicing manager, these accessible and concise publications offer proven advice for carrying out a specific developmental task or solving a specific leadership problem. Ideas Into Action titles include:

Feedback That Works: How to Build and Deliver Your Message
Keeping Your Career On Track: Twenty Success Strategies
Reaching Your Development Goals
Learning from Life: Turning Life's Lessons into Leadership Experience

    Please visit www.ccl.org/publications.

    For more information on CCL's practice areas or special research that may help you in developing solutions for your organization's issues, please call CCL Client Services, (336) 545-2810, e-mail to info@leaders.ccl.org, or visit www.ccl.org.

More About Leadership Issues for Women and Leading in the Context of Difference

The Center for Creative Leadership has had a long-standing interest in the experiences of women leaders. This work is part of the Leading in the Context of Difference group, one of five practice areas at CCL. The overall work of this group is to develop the capacities to lead when the orientations of leaders and those they deal with do not arise from a common set of assumptions. It encompasses the leadership issues of not only women but also African Americans and those from different nations and cultures. This book addresses the unique challenges of high-achieving women by providing five themes for developing women personally and professionally.

Additional activities that relate to the work on women's leadership issues that may be of further interest include:

Publications (available at www.ccl.org/publications)

- *Learning from Life: Turning Life's Lessons into Leadership Experience*, Marian N. Ruderman and Patricia J. Ohlott.
- *Managerial Promotion: The Dynamics for Men and Women*, Marian N. Ruderman, Patricia J. Ohlott, and Kathy E. Kram.
- *Gender Differences in the Development of Managers: How Women Managers Learn from Experience*, Ellen Van Velsor and Martha W. Hughes-James.
- *Making Diversity Happen: Controversies and Solutions*, Ann M. Morrison, Marian N. Ruderman, and Martha W. Hughes-James.
- *Diversity in Work Teams: Research Paradigms for a Changing Workplace*, Susan E. Jackson and Marian N. Ruderman (Eds.).
- *Breaking the Glass Ceiling: Can Women Reach the Top of America's Largest Organizations?*, Ann M. Morrison, Randall

P. White, Ellen Van Velsor, and the Center for Creative Leadership.

- "Single-Gender and Single-Race Leadership Development Programs: Concerns and Benefits," Patricia J. Ohlott and Martha W. Hughes-James. *Leadership in Action*, *17*(4), 1997.

- "How Managers View Success: Perspectives of High-Achieving Women," Marian N. Ruderman, Patricia J. Ohlott, Kate Panzer, and Sara N. King. *Leadership in Action*, *18*(6), 1999.

- "Change and Leadership Development: The Experience of Executive Women," Patricia J. Ohlott. *Leadership in Action*, *19*(5), 1999.

- "Putting Some Life into Your Leadership," Marian N. Ruderman and Patricia J. Ohlott. *Leadership in Action*, *20*(5), 2000.

- "Getting Real: How to Lead Authentically," Marian N. Ruderman and Sharon Rogolsky. *Leadership in Action*, *21*(3), 2001.

Open-Enrollment Program (call 336-545-2810 or visit www.ccl.org/programs for more information)

The Women's Leadership Program (TWLP) explores leadership development issues specifically faced by women and was a key source of information for this book. For middle-level to executive-level women managers, this program creates a safe environment where a woman can bring her whole self to understand and work on the forces that influence her career.

Further Research (contact Marian Ruderman at ruderman@leaders.ccl.org for more information)

Two new research projects are currently under way. One, being conducted with both men and women, replicates a piece of the research discussed in this book. A second, entitled "Leadership Across Differences: Reconciling Ethnicity, Religion, Gender, and Culture," looks at the role of leadership in organizations where there are groups of people who harbor tension, distrust, and antipathy for other groups in their workplace.